KUNGL. VITTERHETS
HISTORIE OCH ANTIKVITETS AKADEMIENS

HANDLINGAR

Antikvariska serien
trettioandra delen

A Chorological Study of North European Rock Art

By Mats P. Malmer

Almqvist & Wiksell International, Stockholm, Sweden

Printed with grants from The Swedish Council for Research in the Humanities and Social Sciences

ISBN 91-7402-110-9
ISSN 0083-6761

Printed in Sweden 1981
Borgströms Tryckeri AB

Foreword

The present study is based on a manuscript finished in January 1972, but never published as other work intervened. As I revised the text I concentrated on the nineteen main geographcial areas into which North European rock art has been divided. Discussion of individual rock art sites included in the earlier manuscript has been omitted here. Work published since 1972 has been used as described in chapter 3.

The illustrations and diagrams have been drawn by Brita Malmer with additions by Roger Blidmo of Stockholm. The text has been translated by Eva Wilson and Simon Wilson of London.

During the course of this work I have benefitted from discussions with most of the specialists in rock art in Scandinavia and of many on the Continent.

I am deeply grateful to all these people, who in different ways have helped me in this task.

Lidingö, 8th October 1980

Mats P. Malmer

Contents

List of illustrations

List of tables

1. Introduction

The study of rock art emerged early as a particular speciality of Scandinavian Archaeology (Åberg 1839. Holmberg 1848). From the beginning there was a strong bias towards an interpretative treatment of the subject. This is easy to understand, since the main feature of rock art is that it represents a desire by prehistoric man to *express* something about this world, his achievements, his beliefs; exactly what, we do not know, but this expression is a message to fellow men or to superhuman beings. It is also understandable that chronological studies, which play such an important role in other areas of archaeology, seem less attractive to research workers engaged in the study of rock art, where closed finds and stratigraphy, the most important means of dating in conventional archaeology, are rarely found.

It is more difficult to explain why students of rock art have failed to carry out the chorological studies which constitute an important part of other archaeological research. Chorological information is always a sound basis for—and often a prerequisite condition of—chronological discussion and cultural-historical interpretation. An archaeological distribution map must never be interpreted as reflecting a static situation; it nearly always represents movement in at least one direction. Archaeological literature has too often seen a new idea or an innovation as striking an area (even of the size of Scandinavia) with the speed of lightning, affecting simultaneously all its different areas. This can never have been true: every archaeological type was first produced by one person living in a certain place at a certain time; thence the new idea spread to his immediate neighbourhood, and from there in ever-increasing circles, until it eventually reached the limits of our distribution map. Therefore, in order to establish a chronology and an interpretation it is necessary to analyse the process of innovation and the direction in which it spread. It is obvious that similar economic, technical, social, religious and other conditions may at times have led to the creation of similar (if never completely identical) types in different places. But even in such cases the centres of innovation, and the spread of ideas from them, will have to be defined. Research into rock art has, however, almost invariably regarded its material as a homogeneous whole, especially where the South Scandinavian engravings are concerned. There has been no research into the influence of the rock art of one area on that of another, nor into the ways in which such an influence might operate.

Rock art is, in fact, particularly well suited to chorological studies. Rock-engravings and rock-paintings are numerous in large areas of Scandinavia, Finland and Karelia. It is probably true to say that no other North European prehistoric artefact has such a rich variety of typological elements and such a wide area of distribution, while at the same time occuring in such large numbers. Furthermore, unlike all other artefacts, rock art has the valuable feature of being immobile—unconditionally so when it occurs on outcrops of rock, but in practice also when it is found on boulders and loose stones; there can be no question of importation. Rock-carvings and rock-paintings never give a false chronological or cultural picture—they are a genuine expression of the culture of the period when they were produced in the area in which they are found.

This thesis may be qualified only by postulating the existence of travelling rock artists. It is obvious that the knowledge of individual rock art motifs was usually disseminated through personal contact. The high artistic quality of many rock-carvings—for instance those found on the numerous sites in Bohuslän—demonstrate that they were made by skilled and talented artists. However, local variations—rarely taken sufficiently into account in past studies—would suggest that the area of activity of such masters never approached even the size of today's smaller administrative regions, such as a *län* or *fylke*. The carvers of rune stones in the Viking Age, later counterparts of the rock artists, confined their activities to quite limited areas, although their skill was doubtless more exclusive and difficult to learn, and therefore presumably less common.

The purpose of the present study is, in short, to investigate the differences between the various North European rock art areas on the basis of the most common motifs and the variations in type that they display. It is to be hoped that the chorological results may be used to reach conclusions about chronology, innovations patterns and interpretation, in particular the probability that the motifs may have been invested with diverse meanings in the different parts of the huge North European region, with its disparate geographical character.

2. Terminology

2.1. General terms

The term *rock art* (Swedish: *bergkonst*) is used here in a broad sense to include both *rock-engravings* (*bergristningar*) and *rock-paintings* (*bergmålningar*). The use of the term 'art' does not imply a commitment to the hypothesis that these designs were primarily aesthetic in inspiration.

For methodological reasons it is necessary to distinguish between rock art and designs found in stone cists; the terms *burial art* (*gravkonst*) and *engravings in burials* (*gravristningar*) may be used.

Since a general term is needed, *petroglyph* (hällristning) may be used to encompass both rock-engravings and engravings in burials.

The terminology used in the study of rock art in Northern Europe has been considerably complicated by the fact that representations of wild animals predominate in northern areas, whereas in the south other motifs (especially ships) are most common. The reason for this polarisation is obvious: in prehistoric Northern Europe, hunting and farming were the primary means of subsistence, the former being predominant in the north, and the latter in the south. However, most of the motifs which occur in North European rock art are so widely distributed that their significance must have varied at least to some extent from one region to another.

The following terms would seem to be the most suitable: *hunting rock-engravings* (*fångstristningar*) and *farming rock-engravings* (*jordbruksristningar*). It must be emphasized, however, that the term farming rock engraving is not applied solely to agricultural motifs, to engravings made by farmers, or, indeed to engravings found in good farming areas. The hunting rock-engravings have a closer, but not exclusive, connection with hunters and their territories. But it is also possible that hunters would engrave designs other than those of their prey in an attempt to ensure the success of the hunt. Thus the terms may be defined as follows: *Scandinavian farming rock-engravings* are those with motifs which originate in a southern agricultural environment. *Scandinavian hunting rock-engravings and rock-paintings* are those which originate in a northern hunting environment. Some motifs arising in an area of mixed hunting and farming economy may contain elements of both types; a clear-cut definition cannot, in fact, be arrived at. The mixture of hunting and farming motifs thus reflects the prevailing economic situation.

A chorological study, being essentially quantitative, requires units which can be measured. Our most important unit is the single design (or figure), which may be defined thus: An *engraved design* (or a *painted design* or an *engraved design in a burial*) is any representation of a human figure, animal, object or any abstract or unidentifiable motif. Scenes consisting of two or more human figures, animals or objects, may be counted as a single design if the engraved (or painted) lines or surfaces which make up the different elements of the scene are continous (as, for instance, in the case of a ship with its crew, or a ploughman with plough and draught-animal).

To render this definition workable, a list of existing *motifs* must be compiled, including all those scenes which are here defined as single designs. Although our definition stipulates that the elements of a scene must be connected in order that it be regarded as a single design, this does not, of course, mean that each figure must consist of a single continous line or surface; circular patterns, for instance, may include concentric circles or dots (fig. 22:6–10), and the same applies to the typical scene of a cart and draught-animal, where the wheels obviously form an integral part of the design (fig. 16). Neither does our definition imply that the creator of such designs never intended unconnected figures to form integrated scenes. The important problems posed by such scenes have not been considered in adequate depth in previous studies. Too often subjective judgments have been made to the effect that two or more figures in close proximity constitute a scene. A more objective assessment could be arrived at through statistical investigation (using automatic data processing) of the relative positions between different motifs on the rock surfaces; and, indeed, such work is already in progress. But the study of such scenes falls outside the scope of the present investigation.

The motifs are further divided into *types* and *sub-types,* according to variations in technique and detail. No strict distinction is made here between these two terms, the use of one or the other being dictated entirely by the demands of textual clarity. All systems of classification used here are *declensions;* thus the symbols retain their significance in whatever order or combination they appear (Malmer 1963, pp 114–119, 269). The declension classification system has logical and mnemotechnical advantages over a rigid system, and also renders the processing of large numbers of typological elements considerably more efficient and rapid. Each symbol, or combination of symbols, is equal to any other symbol; it simply represents a number of designs which have certain specific features identified by the symbols. We can therefore speak of type A and also of type AIa1. While type AIa1 is a sub-type of type A, it is also a sub-type of type I, type a and type 1; it is also a sub-type of types AI, Aa, A1, Ia, I1 and a1 and finally a sub-type of types AIa, AI1, Aa1 and Ia1.

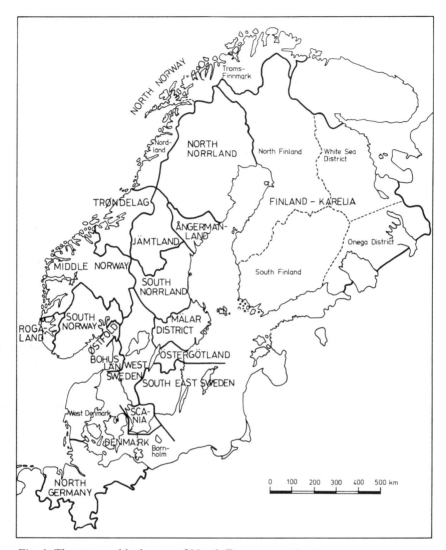

Fig. 1. The geographical areas of North European rock art.

2.2. Geographical terms

The present study covers the rock art of North Germany, Denmark, Sweden, Norway, Finland and Karelia. This area, which may be called *Northern Europe* (fig. 1), is fairly cohesive and well defined. The recent discovery of rock-paintings in Finland serves to link the rock-engravings of Karelia with Scandinavia, while no considerable concentrations of rock art occur beyond Lake Onega until east of the Urals. The North German rock-engravings are similarly linked with South Scandinavian engravings, since the nearest rock art site of any size to the south lies in the region of the Alps.

The rather uneven distribution of rock art in the area investigated produced difficulties in the construction of qualitative maps (e.g. point symbol maps). Quantitative maps (e.g. isarithm maps) are also impractical, as it is difficult to establish suitable reduction values in such a culturally heterogenous area (Malmer 1962, pp. 697–702). Our chorological study must thus be primarily statistical and tabular in approach. A strict division into geographical areas is therefore necessary.

The principles of this division are as follows: the limits of the areas normally follow administrative boundaries. Where rock art is common, and therefore usually well published, the smaller administrative areas and provinces (*amt, fylke* and *landskap*) constitute separate areas (e.g. Bohuslän, Østfold and Rogaland). Where rock art is rare, and less well published, administrative units are joined to form larger areas (e.g. West Sweden and South Norway). The area names have been specially conceived for this study, and do not always conform to common usage; thus the area of South Norrland includes the province of Dalarna, although this is commonly referred to as part of the larger unit of Svealand.

The boundaries of the areas are listed below. The main areas are numbered 1–19; Denmark, North Norway and Finland-Karelia are further subdivided.

(1)   *North Germany.* Schleswig-Holstein, Niedersachsen, Hamburg, Bremen and Mecklenburg.
(2)   *Denmark.*
(2a) *West Denmark.* Denmark to the west of the Sound (i.e. the whole of Denmark except Bornholm).
(2b) *Bornholm.*
(3)   *Scania.*
(4)   *South-East Sweden.* The provinces of Blekinge, Småland, Öland and Gotland.
(5)   *Östergötland.*
(6)   *The Mälar District.* The provinces of Södermanland, Närke, Västmanland and Uppland.
(7)   *South Norrland.* The provinces of Dalarna, Gästrikland, Hälsingland and Medelpad.
(8)   *Jämtland.* The provinces of Jämtland and Härjedalen.
(9)   *Ångermanland.*
(10) *North Norrland.* The provinces of Västerbotten, Norrbotten and Lappland.
(11) *West Sweden.* The provinces of Halland, Västergötland, Dalsland and Värmland.
(12) *Bohuslän.*
(13) *Østfold.*
(14) *South Norway.* The *fylken* of Akershus, Oslo, Buskerud, Vestfold, Telemark, Aust-Agder and Vest-Agder.
(15) *Rogaland.*
(16) *Middle Norway.* The *fylken* of Hordaland, Bergen, Sogn og Fjordane, Møre og Romsdal, Oppland and Hedmark.
(17) *Trøndelag.* The *fylken* of Sør-Trøndelag and Nord-Trøndelag.

(18) *North Norway.*

(18a) *Nordland.*

(18b) *Troms-Finnmark.* The *fylken* of Troms and Finnmark.

(19) *Finland-Karelia.*

(19a) *South Finland.* The provinces of Åland, Finland proper, Nyland, Satakunda, Tavastland, Savolaks and Finnish Karelia.

(19b) *North Finland.* The provinces Österbotten, Finnish Västerbotten and Lappland.

(19c) *The Onega District.* The southern part of Russian Karelia.

(19d) *The White Sea District.* The northern part of Russian Karelia.

Rock art is absent, or occurs to an insignificant extent, in areas (7) South Norrland, (10) North Norrland and (19b) North Finland.

3. Method and material

3.1. Method

The author has studied rock art sites in West Denmark, Bornholm, Scania, Blekinge, Östergötland, Södermanland, Uppland, Bohuslän, Härjedalen, Ångermanland, Østfold, Oslo, Rogaland, Troms, Finnmark and Nyland. Although a considerable number of designs have been examined, they represent only a fraction of the body of material available. The ideal basis for a chorological study would obviously be a new record of all North European rock art by means of a standardised and objective method. However, it seems unlikely that a complete re-registration will be carried out within the foreseeable future; and such a scheme does not, in any case, fall within the scope of the present study. A comprehensive view of the whole North European region can be obtained only by means of the literature. To a certain extent this is facilitated by the amount of literature available, but the very varied nature of the publications from different regions produces considerable difficulties. The areas best served are those where modern corpus-type publications aim to provide a comprehensive survey. In other areas, however, authors have not attempted comprehensive coverage and have selected for description and illustration only such sites and designs as they, for whatever reason, have found interesting; this situation inevitably poses methodological problems.

Ten selected motifs are discussed in this study; taken together they represent at least 95 % of the total number of designs found in North European rock art (excluding cup-marks). Thus, for example, the engravings at Himmelstalund 50, Östergötland (Nordén 1925 A, pl. 51–52), comprise a total of over 300 designs (excluding cup-marks); of these, only six were not catalogued and classified in this study. The designs which were left out are a couple of frame patterns and some possibly damaged symbolic signs. The inclusion of these few designs, which make up the remaining few percent of the total number of figures, would have raised severe difficulties of classification, which (as well as taking up a great deal of space) would not have made a corresponding contribution to this chorological discussion.

The ten motifs are discussed in a sequence designed to throw the chorological aspect into the greatest relief, starting with the ships. These are the commonest motif, and are characterised by relatively small, but distinctive variations. The amount of material is so large that it guarantees a considerable statistical reliability. Any significant qualitative and quantitative differences between areas in Northern Europe, revealed through the analysis of this material, may be used as a basic pattern against which may be measured the distribution of less common motifs.

The main body of material in this study consists of about 9500 figures known to the author before 1972, all accurately defined North European rock art designs. In each design an average of four typological elements were identified; thus the total number of registered and processed elements is about 40,000.

After 1972 some important new publications appeared, particularly Gro Mandt's corpus for Hordaland (1972); two volumes on Kville *härad,* Bohuslän, by Åke Fredsjö, Jarl Nordbladh and Jan Rosvall (1971 and 1975); Göran Burenhult's corpus (1973) of rock-engravings in Götaland (except Bohuslän and Dalsland); and Einar Kjellén and Åke Hyenstrand's work on Uppland (1976). Statistics based on this new literature could, of course, have been substituted for the corresponding section of my 1972 manuscript, which was based on older, inferior and less comprehensive publications. It seemed, however, more interesting from a methodological point of view to juxtapose the old and new literature, and in this way test one of the principal methodological tenets of the present study; namely the use of material from publications of varying scope and accuracy.

The author concentrated on positive identifications, and thus avoided making interpretative decisions about indistinct, shallow cut, or weathered designs. As an overwhelmingly large number of designs are plain and unambiguous it seemed methodologically correct not to compromise the reliability of the results in an attempt to interpret patterns which will perhaps always remain unclear.

The author carried out all the registration and classification himself; the statistical calculations were also performed manually by the author, his only technical aid being an electronic calculator. Automatic data processing was not considered appropriate, as the time saved during the actual calculations would presumably have been lost in programming. But the use of automatic data processing is nonetheless recommended if the data are to be used in any future rock art study project, and the classification symbols have throughout been designed to be compatible with such processes.

3.2. Source literature

The material on which the author based his work may be found in the literature listed below according to region. More recent publications, from which controls for certain areas have been taken, are indicated separately. The name of the author and the date are given in the same way as in the bibliography.

(1) *North Germany*. Capelle 1972.
(2) *Denmark*. Glob 1969.
(3) *Scania*. Althin 1945. Lidén 1938.—Control: Burenhult 1973.
(4) *South-East Sweden*. Arne 1917. Hasselrot-Ohlmarks 1966. Kjellmark-Lindsten 1909. Lidén 1938. Nordin 1911. Salomonsson 1958.—Control: Burenhult 1973.
(5) *Östergötland*. Nordén 1925A.—Control: Burenhult 1973.
(6) *The Mälar District*. Almgren 1960. Ekholm 1916, 1921 A, 1921 B and 1922. Friesen 1915. Janson 1960. Kjellén 1960. Montelius 1900. Nordén 1925 B. Schnittger 1922. Simonsson 1960.—Control: Kjellén-Hyenstrand 1976.
(8) *Jämtland*. Hallström 1960.
(9) *Ångermanland*. Hallström 1960.
(11) *West Sweden*. Claesson 1932. Ekhoff 1893. Ewald 1924. Fredsjö 1956. Hallström 1929. Hasselrot-Ohlmarks 1966. Kjellin 1940. Leijonhufvud 1908. Lidén 1938. Schnittger 1911. Schnittger 1922.—Control: Burenhult 1973.
(12) *Bohuslän*. Baltzer 1881–1890 and 1891–1908.—Control: Fredsjö-Nordbladh-Rosvall 1971 and 1975.
(13) *Østfold*. Gjessing 1939. Johansen 1970. Marstrander 1963.
(14) *South Norway*. Coll 1901 and 1902. Engelstad 1934. Fett 1941. Hallström 1938. Marstrander 1941.
(15) *Rogaland*. Hallström 1938. Fett 1941.
(16) *Middle Norway*. Bakka 1966. Bjørlykke 1903. Bjørn 1916. Bøe 1932 and 1940. Christie 1837. Engelstad 1934. Fett 1939. Gjessing 1935 B, 1936 and 1945. Hagen 1969 and 1970. Hallström 1938 and 1960. Lange 1912. Petersen 1933. Rekstad 1910. Schetelig 1908. Skjelsvik-Straume 1957.—Control: Mandt 1972.
(17) *Trøndelag*. Gjessing 1935 A and 1936. Hallström 1938 and 1960. Marstrander 1950, 1953 and 1966. Petersen 1925 and 1926. Rygh 1908, 1910 and 1913.
(18) *North Norway*. Gjessing 1932 and 1936. Hallström 1938 and 1960. Rygh 1908. Simonsen 1958.
(19) *Finland-Karelia*. Erä-Esko 1955. Europaeus 1922. Hallström 1952. Luho 1962 and 1968. Raudonikas 1936 and 1938. Sarvas 1969 and 1970. Savvateev 1967 and 1968.—Additional material: Ojonen 1973. Sarvas and Taavitsainen 1975 and 1976.

4. Ships

4.1. Terminology and classification

First of all it is necessary to define some of the more important typological elements found in ship designs:

The *line of the gunwale* is the upper horizontal limit of the ship. If the ship is represented by a *single* horizontal line, this line is regarded as the gunwale.

The *line of the keel* is the lower horizontal limit of the ship. If the ship is represented by a *single* line, it is regarded as having no keel.

The *end lines* are vertical, oblique or curved lines at the stem and stern, which join the lines of the gunwale and keel to complete the hull.

The *double prow* of type A ships (defined below) is formed either by both gunwale and keel lines extending beyond the end lines (fig. 2, AI right) or by the end line curving inward and creating a concave prow (fig. 4, left). In type B ships the line of the gunwale is forked (fig. 2, BI). In ships of types C–E, the end lines form concavities centred on vertical (fig. 2, CI) or horizontal (fig. 2, DII left) tangents. The expression 'double prow' obviously does not conform to accepted nautical terminology, but the constructions portrayed in rock-engravings of ships do not conform to constructions found in any known ships.

A *single prow* indicates *either* the continuation of the line of the gunwale or the keel (but not both) beyond the end line (fig. 2, AIII), *or,* in the case of ships with gunwale only, that this line is not forked (fig. 2, BIII). Ships are *also* said to have a single prow when both gunwale and keel lines finish at the end line, and the end line continues above the level of the gunwale (fig. 2, EIII).

A *hammered-out hull* is a hull where the surface between the gunwale and the keel has been removed—or in other words, where the hammered-out surface of the hull is at least twice the width of the lines which make up the prow (fig. 2, C).

A *contoured hull* is a hull where the line of the gunwale, with its extension into the prow, the keel line (but not necessarily the keel's extension beyond the end lines) and the end lines themselves, form a closed outline (fig. 2, D).

The *crew* is represented by two or more parallel lines meeting the gunwale from above at right or acute angles (fig. 3, a); in the latter case the lines representing the crew incline towards the stem of the vessel (fig. 4).

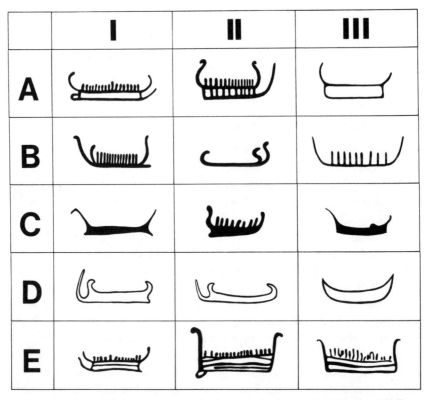

	I	**II**	**III**

Fig. 2. The type-defining elements of ship designs. Series A–E (horizontal lines, hull) and I–III (prows).

(All the illustrations in this book are taken from existing rock-engravings, but they are not drawn to a uniform scale.

Sites: *AI*a1: Åmøy, Rogaland. *AII*a2: Tose, Bohuslän. *AIII*c1: Himmelstalund, Östergötland. *BI*a1: Lökeberget, Bohuslän. *BII*c1: Backa in Brastad, Bohuslän. *BIII*a1: Helgerød, Østfold. *CI*c1: Leonardsberg, Östergötland. *CII*a1: Backa in Brastad, Bohuslän. *CIII*b1: Himmelstalund, Östergötland. *DI*c1: Åmøy, Rogaland. *DII*c1: Åmøy. *DIII*c1: Åmøy. *EI*a1: Berg, Östergötland. *EII*a1: Åmøy, Rogaland. *EIII*b1: Åmøy.)

The *head* is the rounded terminal which sometimes occurs at the top of individual lines which represent the crew (fig. 4).

The *ribs* are those lines which connect the gunwale to the keel, provided that they are not end lines, and that they join the gunwale and keel lines at angles between 60° and 90° (fig. 3:2).

The ship designs show a considerable number of variations, but the main elements, which are subject to variation, are few:

Horizontal lines (number and sheer);

The prows (single or double, height, concavity, and ornament);

The crew; and

The ribs.

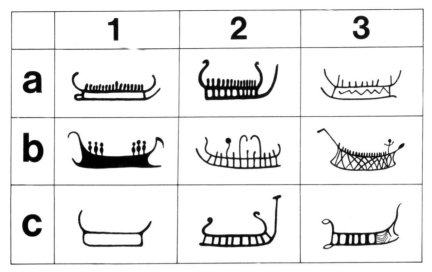

Fig. 3. The type-defining elements of ship designs. Series a–c (crew) and 1–3 (ribs, hull decoration).
(Sites: AI*a1:* Åmøy, Rogaland. AII*a2:* Tose, Bohuslän. AI*a3:* Ekensberg, Östergötland. CI*b1:* Himmelstalund, Östergötland. AI*b2:* Skjeberg, Østfold. AI*b3:* Himmelstalund, Östergötland. AIII*c1:* Himmelstalund. AI*c2:* Madsebakke, Bornholm. AI*c3:* Himmelstalund, Östergötland.)

These elements are well suited to a declension classification system (2.1) using abstract symbols. In the terminology listed below, the four groups of typological elements are assigned upper case letters, Roman numerals, lower case letters and Arabic numerals respectively.

A   Ships with a gunwale and a keel (double-line ships).
B   Ships with a gunwale but no keel (single-line ships).
C   Ships with a hammered-out hull.
D   Contoured ships.
E   Ships with a gunwale and a keel and at least one intermediate horizontal line on the hull.
 I   Ships with two double prows.
 II   Ships with one double and one single prow.
III   Ships with two single prows.
 a   Ships with crew, which sometimes have heads, but (apart from ornamented prows) no other feature above the gunwale (e.g. more detailed human figures or trumpet-like designs).
 b   Ships with designs (in addition to crew) above the gunwale.
 c   Ships with neither crew nor other designs above the gunwale.
 1   Ships with no ribs; the hull may have a hammered-out surface or one or more horizontal lines, but no other lines or designs in the area circumscribed by the gunwale, keel and end lines.
 2   Ships where the hull is decorated exclusively with ribs.
 3   Ships where the hull is decorated with designs other than ribs and/or more horizontal lines.

Fig. 4. The ship-design on the Rørby sword. (Photo: Bertil Centerwall).

The above list serves as an index defining the symbols A, B, C, D, E, I, II, III, a, b, c, 1, 2 and 3. There is no differentiation in status between these symbols; all are of equal importance, both *a priori* and in the opinion of the author.

The symbols may also be regarded as representing types. Thus, for example, type A includes all ships with two horizontal lines (i.e. gunwale and keel) and type III includes all ships with single prows: these types overlap. If, therefore, mutually exclusive types are to be defined, capable of embracing all ship designs found in rock art, the symbols must be combined to form a typological system of four symbols, one from each of the groups of elements A–E, I–III, a–c and 1–3.

Theoretically this system has a capacity of 135 mutually exclusive types. But, because the characteristics represented by 2 and 3 are incompatible with B and C, the real capacity is $3 \times 27 + 2 \times 9$, which totals 99 types; a sufficient number to produce an outline survey of the North European ship designs. The flexibility of the system also makes it easier to memorize the characteristics of the ninety-nine types—which would hardly have been possible with a rigid classification system.

Figs. 2 and 3 demonstrate the construction of the system (the illustrations are taken from existing rock-engravings). Practical difficulties prevent a diagrammatic representation of all the ninety-nine types; fig. 2, therefore, only illustrates the complete range of variations of the horizontal lines (types A–E) and the prows (types I–III) while the examples of

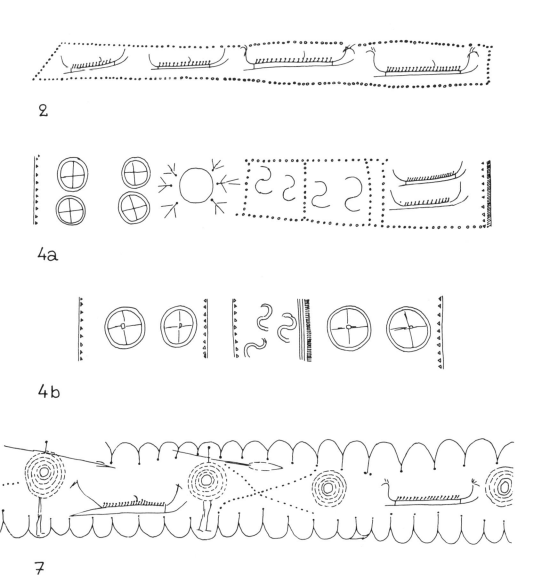

Fig. 5. Designs on the Wismar trumpet. Decoration zones number 2, 4 and 7, counting from the bell. (Drawings from the original by Brita Malmer.)

variations involving the crew (types a–c) and ribs (types 1–3) are incidental. In fig. 3 the emphasis is reversed and the complete range of variations of the two latter groups (a–c and 1–3) are illustrated, while examples of the former (A–E and I–III) occur only incidentally.

To complete the diagram it may be imagined that in fig. 2 each of the squares in columns A, D and E are subdivided into nine squares (corresponding to fig. 3) and that each of the squares in columns B and C are subdivided into three squares (corresponding to fig. 3, column 1).

4.2. The logical sequence of the classification system and its hypothetically chronological application

Within the groups the typological elements have been arranged as far as possible according to their degree of similarity:

I, two double prows. II, one double and one single prow. III, two single prows.

a, Lines representing crew, but no other designs above the gunwale. b, other designs, possibly together with crew, above the gunwale. c, no designs above the gunwale.

1, no ribs or other designs on the hull. 2, ribs, but no other designs on the hull. 3, other designs, possibly together with ribs, on the hull.

The determining factor in deciding which element should be placed first in each short series was the appearence of what are probably the earliest of the ship designs which can be dated with any reasonable accuracy, those found on the Rørby sword (fig. 4) and the Wismar trumpet (fig. 5); the representations of ships on the second stone slab in the Kivik grave were presumably also of this type (fig. 6). The arrangements of the gunwale and keel in these designs have therefore been assigned the symbol A, and the complete designation for these designs is AIa1. The elements B–E can all be seen as modifications of A, but they cannot be arranged in sequence.

Fig. 2 demonstrates clearly that the designs in the horizontal column A and the vertical column I show a greater similarity to AI than the eight designs in the squares below and to the right. It is therefore possible to hypothecate a date for the origin of these design type thus:

AI is the earliest.

BI, CI, DI, EI, AII and AIII are later.

BII, CII, DII, EII, BIII, CIII, DIII and EIII are the latest.

Similarly fig. 3 gives rise to the following hypothesis:

a1 is the earliest.

b1, c1, a 2 and a3 are later.

b2, c2, b3 and c3 are the latest.

A comparison of this kind cannot however provide any information concerning the length of time the older types may have *survived*.

4.3. Other classification systems

Ekholm's (1916) classification system was based partly on a chorological study in Uppland. Single-line ships (type B in the present study) are referred to the same period as double-line ships (type A).

Schnittger (1922) argues that the single-line ships are older than the double-line ships, because the former are more 'primitive'.

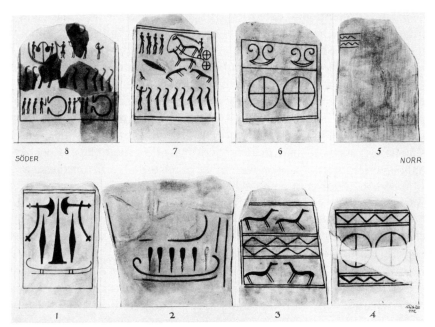

Fig. 6. The eight decorated stone slabs from the Kivik grave. (Wash-drawing by H. Faith-Ell.)

Gjessing (1935 A, pp. 127, 132) also places the single-line ships first in the chronological sequence. On the site Bardal, Beitstaden parish, Nord-Trøndelag, Gjessing observed that where single-line and doubleline ships cross, the latter are nearly always more deeply cut; he therefore inferred that they were of later date. But a deep line cutting through a shallower line does not in itself indicate a stratigraphical relationship. If, however, a shallow line could be seen to have made an impression in a deeper cut at the place where the two lines cross, it would imply a definite chronological relationship and the shallower line would obviously be of later date.

Althin (1945, pp. 47, 156–169) refutes the suggestion that the Scandinavian single-line ships derive from West-European chamber-tomb engravings. His thesis, that the original form of the Scandinavian ship designs must have been a double-line ship, is methodologically important.

The classification system published by Eva and Per Fett (1941, pl. 82) is characterized by a notable clarity and capacity. It differs, however, from a declension classification system in that the numerals 1–3 mean one thing when combined with the letters A–G, and another in combination with the letters J–K.

Marstrander (1963, pp. 76–77 and pl. 64) strongly stressed the importance of stylistic considerations. Almgren, too (1964, p. 158, and 1970) declared his intention to date rock art by its style. Stylistic studies differ from other branches of typological research in that the scholar initially forms an intuitive interpretation of the stylistic intentions of the pre- historic artist. However, a scientific stylistic investigation demands an analysis of the basis for such intuitive impressions, and a recognition and definition of the relevant typological elements. The more rich and com- plex the art, the more useful are these intuitive impressions (in the study of styles such as baroque and rococo, for example); but in the case of simpler art, accurate analytical methods must take their place. Rock art, although rich by comparison with other prehistoric North European art, is of course in this context poor.

Gro Mandt's classification system (1972, pp. 14–16, 55–60) was pub- lished only after the manuscript of the present study was completed. Her classifications are fundamentally very similar to the system presented here, but it is a hierarchical system, not a declension. Only two main types are recognized, the single-line ship (type I) and the doubleline ship (type II). The common type C of the present study was not distinguished as a separate type, for the simple reason that it is rare in western Norway. Crew and ribs were not expressed by symbols and were not subject to statistical processing.

In a survey of Danish rock-carvings, published after the completion of the present study, Rostholm (1972, p. 19) recognizes four of our hull types arranged in the sequence B, A, E and C. Chronologically the double-line ships are placed first; and there is an excellent quantitative and chorological survey.

4.4. The chorology and chronology of the corpus

This corpus consists of 3877 classified ship designs: 72 from Denmark, 2381 from Sweden, 1289 from Norway and 135 from Finland-Karelia. No ship designs occur in North Germany. It is impossible to tell how far these figures reflect the actual proportion of ship designs that survive. It seems likely, however, that Denmark is represented comparatively com- prehensively, due to the recent, excellently illustrated publication of all known rock-engravings in this area. The number of ship designs in Denmark is therefore likely to become proportionately even smaller in the course of time.

Table 1 shows the distribution of the ship designs by type and area. Due to considerations of space, only the sub-types of A–C are included. The vast majority of ship designs occur in a zone of central Scandinavia, from Östergötland in the east (with 645 ship designs) to Bohuslän (1155), Østfold (316) and Rogaland (499) in the west: a total of 2615 ship designs representing at least two thirds of the entire corpus (Table 1 B–E).

The classification system used here has a capacity of $3 \times 27 + 2 \times 9$ or 99 types (4.1). Of these types 78 are actually represented in the corpus. All nine B-types and all nine C-types are represented, and only two A-types are absent (AIIa3 and AIIIa3). Nineteen D-types are represented, but eight are absent, and of the E-types only sixteen are represented, while eleven are absent. The many D- and E-type ship designs which are not represented must to some extent be due to the fact that D- and E-type ships are generally rare.

Table 2 illustrates the frequency with which the fourteen type defining elements (used in the classification system to define the types) occur both within each of the geographical areas and in Northern Europe as a whole. The proportion of each element in the different groups of elements (A–E, I–III, a–c and 1–3) is expressed in percentages in table 3. Element 1 (ships without ribs) has been distributed between ships where ribs are logically possible (A, D and E) and ships which cannot have ribs (B and C). All elements vary greatly in frequency from one area to another. The elements are listed below with their frequency throughout Northern Europe:

I	62 %	C	20 %
a	58 %	II	15.5 %
BC1	50 %	2	15.5 %
A	46 %	b	12.5 %
ADE1	32.5 %	3	2 %
B	30.5 %	D	2 %
c	29.5 %	E	1.5 %
III	22.5 %		

It can be seen that the elements which occur most frequently are indeed the four elements which comprise the hypothetical prototype (AIa1) of the classification system i.e. the Rørby–Wismar–Kivik type (4.2.), although the elements occur in a different sequence, i.e. IaA1 (I, ships with two double prows; a, ships with crew; A, double-line ships and 1, ships without ribs).

The least frequent elements are E (ships with three or more horizontal lines), D (contoured ships), 3 (ships with ribs and other designs on the hull), b (ships with crew and other designs above the gunwale), 2 (ships with ribs) and II (ships with one single and one double prow). These features occur most frequently in those type combinations which on logical grounds are latest (4.2.).

Thus it would seem that those elements which occur most frequently are the earliest, and those which occur least frequently are the latest. If this is indeed true, it may be explained by the greater diversification of the ship motif towards the end of the period in which it was used. This would cause each element then in fashion to occur less frequently.

Features of medium frequency are elements B (single-line ships), c (ships without crew), III (ships with two single prows) and C (ships with a

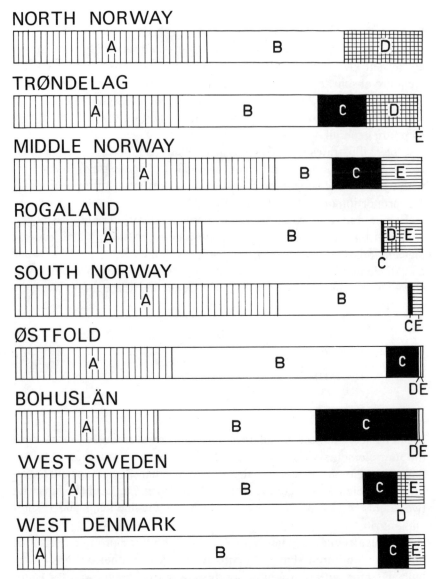

Fig. 7. The frequency of ship design types A–E in nine western areas.

hammered-out hull). By comparison with the least frequent elements, the features of medium frequency can be said to be simpler modifications of the elements of the hypothetical protoype. It seems possible at least that the elements of medium frequency originate somewhere near the middle of the period in which the ship motif was used. But the hypothetical chronological system outlined here clearly needs additional factual supporting evidence before it may be considered proven.

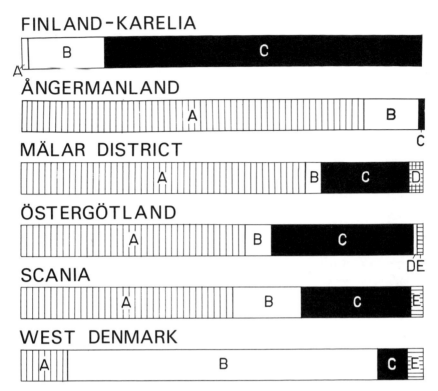

Fig. 8. The frequency of ship design types A–E in six eastern areas.

Table 3 shows that the frequency of the elements varies greatly from one area to another. For example, element A (double-line ships) has a frequency of only 11.5 % in West Denmark, whereas in Rogaland it is as high as 46 %, in Östergötland 55.5 % and in Ångermanland 85 %. On the other hand, element I (ships with two double prows) has a frequency of 90 % in Scania, but only 1 % in Ångermanland. Element B (single-line ships) has a frequency of 77 % in West Denmark and 52.5 % in Østfold, as against only 6.5 % in Östergötland. Element C (ships with a hammaered-out hull) has a frequency of 35.5 % in Östergötland and only 7.5 % in West Denmark and 8 % in Østfold.

The distribution seems confused and may convey the impression of an arbitrary pattern of frequencies which changes from one area to another at random. Is it, then, possible to trace the pattern of the innovation process of the ship motif?

In prehistoric Northern Europe new impulses normally spread northwards from the south, this tendency being particularly marked from the beginning of the Neolithic period. For this reason we shall first examine the possibility that the ship motifs in rock art spread in this way. The distribution pattern of what are probably the earliest fairly accurately dated ship representations (all of type AIa1, i.e. Rørby, West Denmark; Wismar, North Germany and Kivik, Scania), would tend to support the theory of a spread of innovations from south to north.

Type A ship designs (double-line ships) have a frequency of only 11.5 % in West Denmark (the natural innovation centre of Scandinavian Bronze Age culture); this might be seen as an argument against the theory of an innovatory pattern moving north. A distribution pattern is often interpreted thus: the area where a type is best represented is the area where it originated—and in many cases this can be proved to be correct. But sometimes it is patently wrong, as for example in the case of the Corded Ware of the Battle Axe cultures of the Middle Neolithic (Malmer 1962, p. 760 and Tab. 91). In a creative centre (as Denmark has frequently been in the past) a type will not be produced for very long before new impulses (for example from the continent of Europe) cause the creation of new types. But peripheral regions (central and northern Scandinavia were often such regions during the Stone Age and Bronze Age) often lag behind to a considerable extent, so that types may be produced in such areas long after they had gone out of fashion in the central regions. In other words: the spread of the earliest of a series of culturally related types would follow an uninhibited innovation pattern, while the pattern of spread of subsequent types would be more inhibited. The result is that the earliest type is proportionately best represented in peripheral areas.

A preliminary examination seems to suggest that elements A–E, which determine the main design of the hull, vary regionally both from north to south and from east to west. Chorological relationships of this complexity can often best be illustrated in diagramatic form. In figs. 7–10 each area is represented by a horizontal bar, the length of which corresponds to 100 %; the values are taken from table 3.

Fig. 7 shows nine western areas from West Denmark in the south to North Norway. By contrast fig. 8 shows six eastern areas, again beginning at the bottom with West Denmark—on the assumption that this is the innovation centre—and continuing with more northerly areas to finish with Ångermanland and Finland-Karelia at the top.

The two diagrams correspond in that the proportion of type A ships (double-line ships) by-and-large gradually increases from south to north. At the same time the diagrams differ in that ships of type B (single-line ships) are particularly strongly represented in the west, while ships of type C (ships with hammered-out hulls) are correspondingly strongly represented in the east. A third main tendency to emerge from the diagrams is the concentration of unusual ship types—i.e. type D (contoured ships) and type E (ships with three or more horizontal lines)—in Norway, especially in Rogaland and areas to the north.

An apparently confused image has become more explicit with the aid of the diagrams. The most obvious interpretation, as demonstrated by the earliest type (type A), is that we are dealing with an innovation pattern, moving northwards from an area in the south; this diffusion process caused contrasting developments in the areas to the west (type B) and to the east (type C) at a slightly later stage. During the final stage, localised forms (types D and E) seem to have developed, especially in the north-west.

The increased proportion of ship designs of type A in areas to the north does not in itself justify the conclusion that the direction of the innovation trend was from the south towards the north; it could just as well have gone in the opposite direction. Some further indications, however, favour an innovation pattern in a northerly direction:

1) If the direction of the diffusion process was from north to south, we have to postulate a very large and scattered innovation centre, including North Norway and Trøndelag as well as the Mälar District (the role of Ångermanland being uncertain). West Denmark, on the other hand, represents an innovation centre of suitable size.

2) As the type A ship designs occur in West Denmark no later than the transition between Montelius' periods 1 and 2 of the Bronze Age, an innovation pattern from north to south would imply that the designs originated very early in North Norway and the Mälar District.

3) Probably the earliest ship designs which can be dated with any certainty are found in the south: i.e. Rørby, Wismar and Kivik.

4) The innovation patterns of prehistoric farming cultures—and not least those of the Bronze Age—usually begin in the south, in West Denmark.

5) If the innovations started in North Norway and spread strongly southwards into Denmark, why then did the process not continue further south into North Germany? A movement from south to north better explains the southern boundary of the ship motif.

There are two exceptions to the general tendency for type A ships to be better represented in the northernmost of two adjacent areas; fig. 7 shows that Rogaland has a smaller proportion of type A ships than South Norway and that Trøndelag has a smaller proportion of these designs than Middle Norway. These irregularities may be most readily explained if we postulate that Rogaland and Trøndelag acted as secondary innovation centres which received impulses from West Denmark before any other areas; from these centres there was a subsequent diffusion into the larger and poorer areas of South Norway, Middle Norway and North Norway. The same argument also applies to Østfold.

Type C seems to have a more local distribution than both types A and B, and is confined mainly to Scania, Östergötland and the Mälar District. Fig. 10, which shows the situation in South-East Sweden and Bornholm, confirms this interpretation; here types A and B are again predominant.

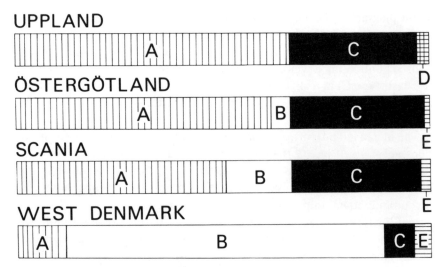

Fig. 9. The frequency of ship design types A–E in four eastern areas.
Control corpus.

The reason why the area of South-East Sweden is seen in conjunction with Bornholm is the fact that the rock-engravings of the former area are concentrated along its south-eastern periphery—thus Blekinge has 34 ship designs and Gotland 23. Only one ship design occurs on Öland and 8 in Småland, through which presumably lay the natural route connecting Scania and Östergötland.

The quantities in which the sub-types are found can presumably also be used for chronological studies. In West Denmark, for instance, there are 11.5 % type A ships of only one type (AIa1); in Rogaland there are 46 % type A ships and 17 types (8 of type AI, 5 of type AII and 4 of type AIII); and in Ångermanland there are 85 % type A ships and 13 types (3 of type AI, 2 of type AII and 8 of type AIII). The figures indicate the improbability of type A ships being produced during the same length of time in the three areas. This would suggest rather that type A ships originated more or less simultaneously in West Denmark and Rogaland, but the motif was discontinued in the former area earlier than in the latter. Type A ships were presumably introduced into Ångermanland later than in Rogaland but probably continued to be used there for a longer period. This may be deduced from the fact that most type A ships found in this area are of a form far removed from the postulated prototype AIa1.

The recognition of an innovation pattern from south to north, and of a contrast between western and eastern areas of Scandinavia, has so far been based on a study of elements A–E only: that is those concerned with horizontal lines. The conclusions would carry more weight if they were

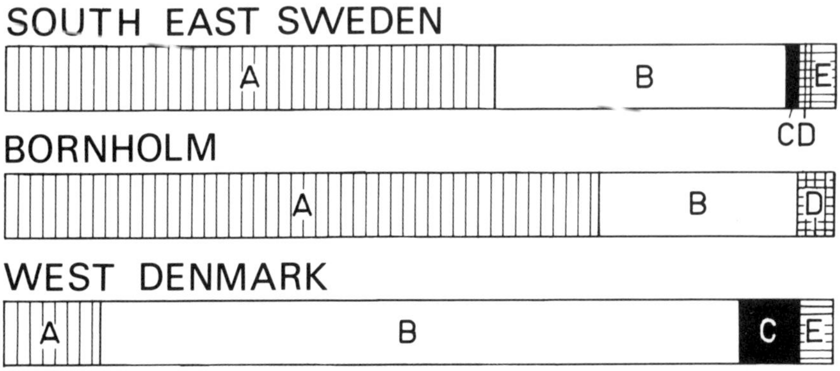

SOUTH EAST SWEDEN

BORNHOLM

WEST DENMARK

Fig. 10. The frequency of ship design types A–E in three south-eastern areas.

based on comparisons between all the seventy-eight types involved. The graphic representation of such large numbers of type frequencies within a number of geographical areas is technically complicated; however, the kind of cumulative diagram which has been extensively used in recent years in the study of Stone Age settlement sites, may perhaps prove useful.

Fig. 11 illustrates how this kind of diagram is constructed: 43 A-, B-and C-ship types represented in the corpus are set off along the horizontal axis with an additional space for types D and E respectively. The 35 D-and E-ship types have not been marked separately, as their combined percentages are so low that the curve would appear virtually horizontal and without any information value, while the whole diagram would be almost twice as big, thus making it more difficult to read.

The percentages are marked off on the vertical axis. Each area is represented by a curve, and the types are marked as points on the curve; the data are based on table 1. The curves are cumulative: this means that values for each individual type are added together. In Bohuslän, for instance, the earliest type is AIa1 with a frequency of 7 %; the next type is AIa2 with 9 % which is thus plotted at the position of 16 %; next is type AIa3 with 0.5 % which is plotted at 16.5 %, and so on.

Fig. 11 demonstrates that cumulative diagrams of this type can produce visually striking results. The diagram illustrates four geographically distant areas, Bohuslän, the Mälar District, Ångermanland and Finland-Karelia, and the curves show conspicuous differences.

Fig. 12 illustrates the cumulative frequency distributions of the four richest and best-published western areas, West Denmark, Bohuslän, Østfold and Rogaland. When compared with fig. 11, it may be seen that the western areas are indeed a closely-knit unit. The section illustrating the distribution of type A ship designs shows clearly that the proportion of type A ships increases gradually in areas further north. The curves

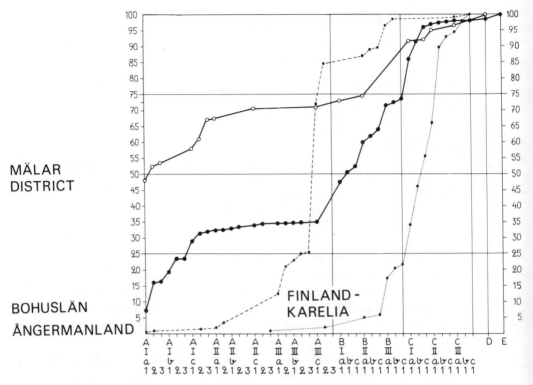

MÄLAR
DISTRICT

BOHUSLÄN

ÅNGERMANLAND

FINLAND -
KARELIA

Fig. 11. Cumulative diagram of the ship design types.

representing Østfold and Rogaland demonstrate that the former has more
ships of type AI, while the latter area has the larger proportion of type A
ships when the three types I–III are all included in the comparison.

Fig. 13 shows a similar diagram of the richest and best-published areas
of the eastern diffusion route: Scania, Östergötland and the Mälar District. The diagram of the eastern areas shows slightly greater differences
than that of the western areas, but it nonetheless represents a cohesive
unit. The greater differences between the curves in fig. 12 is due to the
fact that the process, which causes the percentages of type A ships to
increase in more northerly areas, becomes more pronounced along the
diffusion route in the east than in the west. As far as type A ships are
concerned, the relationship between Scania and Östergötland is similar
to that observed between Østfold and Rogaland; thus there are more
ships of AI design in Scania, but a balance between the two areas is
achieved when types AII and AIII are also taken into account.

The facts discussed so far make it possible to outline the main features
of the innovation pattern of ship designs. The motif originated in West
Denmark at a time approximately indicated by the curved sword from
Rørby, i.e. period 1 (or at least at a time before the introduction of the

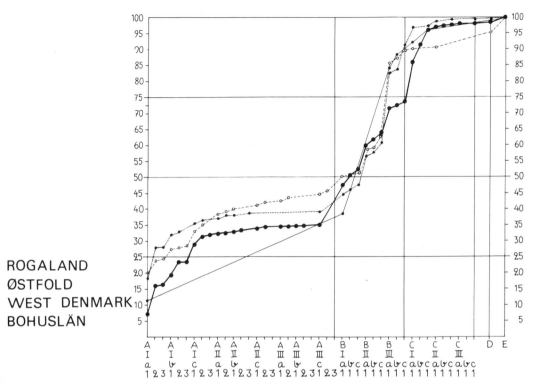

ROGALAND
ØSTFOLD
WEST DENMARK
BOHUSLÄN

Fig. 12. Cumulative diagram of the frequency of ship design types in four western areas.

Scandinavian spiral ornament); its original form was the double-line ship of type AIa1. From West Denmark the ship motif spread fan-wise to other parts of Northern Europe; it is, however, possible to distinguish three main routes of diffusion, a western, an eastern and a south-eastern branch. A common feature of all three routes of diffusion is a strong element of single-line ships (type B). The fact that the proportion of type A ships progressively increases northwards along both the eastern and the western routes would suggest that type B ships also originated in the south, and that their northward spread was inhibited to some extent. There are many type B ships in West Denmark and the origin of the type must be considered to lie in this area. Ships with hammered-out hulls (type C) are peculiar to the eastern branch which consists of the eastern regions of the Swedish mainland: it is unlikely that type C ships originated in West Denmark, as the type is very unevenly distributed along the three routes and only two ships of this type have been found in West Denmark itself. The contoured ships (type D) and ships with three or more horizontal lines on the hull (type E) are peculiar to the Norwegian areas of the western route. It is also unlikely that these types were developed from Danish rock-engravings, but it is possible that they may have their origin in decorated bronze objects of the Danish Late Bronze Age; this will be discussed more fully below (4.6.4).

4.5. Control corpus

4.5.1. Scania

The 112 classified ship designs in the original corpus (table 2) are taken from Althin (1945). The control corpus (table 4) consists of 107 ship designs taken from Burenhult (1973). The quality of the illustrations in both publications is excellent. A comparison between tables 3 and 5 (which represent the type-defining elements of the ship designs) demonstrates that there are only small differences between the two corpuses.

4.5.2. South-East Sweden

The 66 ship designs taken from the original very diverse list of sources have been replaced by a corpus of 211 classified ship designs taken from Burenhult (1973), which is three times as large. It might therefore be expected that a considerable difference would be seen between the original and the control corpuses; however, the proportion of type A ships decreased minimally from 59 % in the original corpus to 57.5 % in the control corpus, while there was an increase in type B ships from 35 % to 38 % and in type C ships from 1.5 % to 4.5 %.

4.5.3. Östergötland

The original corpus consists of 645 ship designs taken from Nordén (1925 A), while 743 ship designs in the control corpus are drawn from Burenhult (1973). The similarities between the two corpuses are considerable; the most important difference is an increase in type A ships from 55.5 % in the original corpus to 61.5 % in the control corpus. Of this 6 % increase, 2 % is due to a re-classification of type B ships and 2.5 % is due to a re-classification of type C ships—this is because some of the designs which were interpreted by Nordén as ships with a hammered-out hull (type C) or as single-line ships (type B), have been shown by Burenhult's more efficient recording methods to be double-line ships (type A). But the preponderance of type C ships in the eastern region, with a particular concentration in Östergötland, remains unchallenged.

4.5.4. Uppland

The original corpus comprises 136 ship designs in the Mälar District, collected from a large number of different sources. The number of known and registered figures has now increased considerably, especially

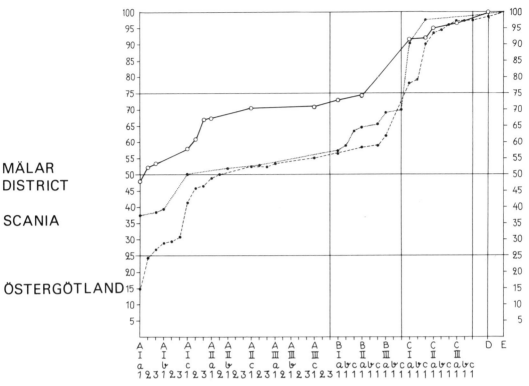

MÄLAR
DISTRICT

SCANIA

ÖSTERGÖTLAND

Fig. 13. Cumulative diagram of the frequency of ship design types in three eastern areas.

through the energetic activities of Einar Kjellén; thus the number of known ship designs in the province of Uppland alone amounts to no less than 1653 (Kjellén-Hyenstrand 1976, p. 117). Uppland now emerges as one of the areas in Northern Europe where rock art occurs most abundantly—although it is likely that intensified research in other areas would greatly increase the volume of known rock art. So far only a small proportion of rock-engravings from Uppland have been illustrated in print: the control corpus consists of 159 ship designs. Tables 3 and 5 show that they group together into types in approximately the same pattern as the 136 ship designs in the original corpus, which represented the whole Mälar District. The increased proportion from south to north of type A ships is represented in the original corpus by the following figures: Scania 52.5 %, Östergötland 55.5 % and the Mälar District 70.5 %. The corresponding figures in the control corpus are: Scania 50.5 %, Östergötland 61.5 % and Uppland 66 %. The evidence of the control corpus, therefore, does not necessitate any modification of a hypothetical south to north innovation pattern. The new figures from Scania, Östergötland and Uppland are represented on the graph fig. 9, which should be compared with fig. 8.

4.5.5. Halland and Västergötland

The original corpus consists of only 47 ship designs taken from a large number of publications, representing the four provinces of Halland, Västergötland, Dalsland and Värmland. The control corpus consists of 38 ship designs from Halland and Västergötland (the other two provinces were not included in Burenhult (1973)). The original corpus and the control corpus correspond well with each other, at least as far as the dominant type in this area (type B) is concerned.

4.5.6. Svenneby and Bottna

The rock-engravings in the two parishes Svenneby and Bottna in Kville *härad,* Bohuslän, have been carefully and comprehensively published by Nordbladh and Rosvall on the basis of Åke Fredsjö's documentation (Fredsjö et al. 1971 and 1975). No less than 539 classified ship designs, taken from these publications, make up a control corpus which can be compared with the 1155 ship designs in the original corpus, all of which were compiled from Baltzer (1881–1908). In his publication, Baltzer paid little attention to Kville *härad* (placing much more emphasis on Tanum *härad*)—the parishes of Svenneby and Bottna were not represented at all. Exceptionally in this case, therefore, the contents of the control corpus is completely different from the original corpus.

A comparison between tables 3 and 5 shows that the two corpuses correspond to the extent that types A and B dominate, while they are both of approximately equal importance. Their dominant position in relation to other designs is, however, more marked in Svenneby and Bottna than in the rest of Bohuslän (as represented in the original corpus).

The disparity between the control corpus compiled from Svenneby and Bottna and the original corpus taken from the rest of Bohuslän, may reflect real or apparent differences according to whether or not there is some element of error in the source material. The most obvious error could lie in some peculiarity of Baltzer's illustration technique: if, for instance, the horizontal lines of double-line ships (type A), were clumsily drawn so close together that some of them take on the appearence of ships with hammered-out hulls (type C).

4.5.7. Hordaland

For the purposes of the original corpus the name Middle Norway was used for an area comprising Hordaland, Bergen, Sogn og Fjordane, Møre og Romsdal, Opland and Hedmark. The literature covering this area is diverse and the 50 ship designs represent only three *fylken*; Hordaland has 4, Sogn og Fjordane 40 and Møre og Romsdal 6 ship designs. The control corpus, compiled from Mandt (1972), represents a considerable increase: there are 107 ship designs from Hordaland alone. It is not surprising, therefore, that a comparison between tables 3 and 5 reveals great differences. On the other hand, the control corpus from Hordaland corresponds well with the original corpus from the neighbouring area to the south, Rogaland, the rock art of which was published (as comprehensively as the material from Hordaland is today) by Fett in 1941. For instance, 46 % type A ships and 44 % type B ships in Rogaland compare with 47.5 % type A and 44 % type B ship designs in Hordaland.

It seems, therefore, that Hordaland belonged to the same innovation area as Rogaland, at least as far as ship designs are concerned. The provinces to the north, Sogn og Fjordane and Møre og Romsdal, appear by contrast as retarded areas—the percentages which apply to this area are almost identical to those given in table 3 and fig. 7 for Middle Norway.

4.6. Detailed chronology

4.6.1. Summary of results

So far the result of this investigation into the chorology and chronology of the ship motif can be summarised as follows: the ship motif first appears in Period 1, probably towards the end of the period (at about the date of the Rørby sword). At this time it takes the form of type A (double-line ships) and it is found in Denmark. From here the ship motif spreads northwards, reaching as far as northernmost Norway. The other ship types, B to E, are of later origin than type A. The evidence points to types B and C being probably contemporary: their distribution is strikingly different, with a predominantly westerly distribution of type B and an easterly distribution of type C. Type I (ships with two double prows) is older than types II and III; type a (ships with crew) is older than types b and c; and type 1 (ships without ribs) is older than types 2 and 3.

4.6.2. Type A ships

The date of the first appearence of type A can be safely assigned to Period 1 or, at the latest, to the beginning of Period 2, since it appears on the curved sword from Rørby (fig. 4); it must in any case be dated to a time before the introduction of the spiral ornament. The Rørby sword is dated by means of the ornament (which relates it to the massive shaft-hole axes of Fårdrup type), by the design of the pommel (which is characteristic of Period 1) and finally by the existence of the curved flint sword from Favrskov on Fyn, which cannot possibly be dated to the beginning of the Late Bronze Age (although such a date has been suggested for the curved swords). It has also been suggested that the sword could have been imported and the ship design added in Scandinavia (Lomborg 1959, p. 117). The technique used in the execution of the ship—both lines and dots—is, however, identical to that used for the rest of the decoration of the sword. (Mathiassen 1957, p. 47. Gräslund 1964, p. 301). Nevertheless, if we postulate that the sword was imported complete with the ship design from, for instance, the region of Hungary—Transylvania, it is difficult to explain the fact that the ship motif, so common in Scandinavian rock-engravings, is absent in that area. It has been argued that the abundance of air bubbles in the metal suggests that curved swords are not of Scandinavian origin, as this is supposedly not characteristic of Scandinavian bronzes. (Lomborg 1959, p. 118). But the metal of those bronzes which, on the basis of their ornamentation are closest in time to the curved swords (i.e. the Fårdrup axes), is often conspicuously flawed (Malmer 1970, p. 209 note 45). Another argument in favour of a Scandinavian origin is the similarity in size between the two swords from Rørby, Sjaelland and that from S. Åby in Scania, which suggests that these swords were made in the same workshop within a short space of time. (Mathiassen 1957, p. 44). The notion that three curved swords from a Hungarian workshop should have been exported to Scandinavia to be found in modern times—while at the same time not a single example of this production has been found on the Continent—is so far fetched that it must be dismissed.

The Rørby ship is drawn with great elegance and skilful stylisation; it is inconceivable that it should be a copy of the much coarser ship engravings on stone. On the other hand, it is also difficult to suppose that the Rørby ship represents a clever artist's first experiment in portraying a Scandinavian ship. In several ways the design is reminiscent of Mediterranean ship representations (Malmer 1970, p. 199. Kjellén-Hyenstrand 1977, p. 63). Therefore a reasonable hypothesis might be that the Rørby ship is a cleverly executed copy of a foreign prototype, and in its turn served as one of the models for ship representations in rock art; or at least one may postulate that it is a characteristic expression of the artistic milieu in which the farming rock-engravings in Northern Europe developed.

The Rørby ship is one of very few engravings on bronze which completely correspond to the definition of the eqivalent rock art motif. It is a completely satisfactory representation of type AIa1. Other bronze engravings in this category are those on the Wismar trumpet. Of eight ship designs on this object, three represent type AIa1 and five type AIb1. In the latter group the designation to type b, instead of type a, is due to the small curved line which occurs above lines representing the crew (fig. 5:2 and 5:7, left). This line must have had special significance; the most obvious explanation is, perhaps, that it portrays a trumpet. It seems clear that the Wismar mounts themselves belonged to a trumpet rather than to a drinking horn.

It seems natural to assign the ornament of the Wismar trumpet to Period 3 in view of the rows of linked spirals; the arguments put forward by Glob also support this dating. (Glob 1969, pp. 49–52). In common with the Rørby ship, the Wismar ships have slanting lines representing the crew, with heads, but the ships differ in that the end lines of the Wismar ships are straight (with one exception) and that the crew are not grouped in pairs; in addition, four of these ships have animal heads of two different designs on the prows. These rather modest differences agree with the suggested difference in date from the transition between Periods 1 and 2 for Rørby to Period 3 for Wismar.

Although the Rørby and Wismar ships demonstrate that the type A ship design was already known in South Scandinavia in the Early Bronze Age (and indeed probably in Period 1), it does not necessarily follow that the type was actually used for rock-engravings at this time. However, by considering the engravings on stone slabs in the grave at Kivik it can be established that this was indeed the case: here the best-preserved of the ship designs (the lower of two ships on stone 2, fig. 6:2) can be identified as representative of type AIa1. Although the stone is weathered and the end lines cannot be distinguished, no other identification is possible. A classification to any of types D–E, II–III or b–c can be disregarded; the only possible alternative to type AIa1 is either AIa2 or AIa3, but these types hardly occur in Scania (table 1A); furthermore the inclusion of the Kivik ship in either type would imply not only that the end lines had weathered away, but also that rib lines and/or other ornaments on the hull had been obliterated. The crew lines do not slant, but have heads, and are thus related to the Rørby and Wismar designs. The Kivik grave is dated to the Early Bronze Age on the basis of the large cist and the cairn. Marstrander's skilful analysis of the bronze fragments found in the grave confirms a probable dating to Period 3 (Marstrander 1963, pp. 331–333).

The chariot, charioteer and two horses on stone 7 in the Kivik grave (fig. 6:7), like the ship design on the Rørby sword, appear to have a Mediterranean inspiration. By what means could Mediterranean art influence the art of the Early Scandinavian Bronze Age? The kind of portable material most likely to have served as prototypes are decorated bronzes, and textiles with woven or embroidered designs. All eight pictures in the Kivik grave have frames, which seem out of place if we consider the designs as ordinary rock-engravings transferred from a rocky outcrop to a stone chamber. The joins between the slabs already separate the representations into groups more distinctly than is usually the case in rock-engravings. These frames may therefore indicate that the designs could have been copied from rectangular decorated cloths. Furthermore, the horizontal divisions on the Kivik slabs are reminiscent of strips of textile. It is true that not even one fragment of cloth found in Scandinavia has been shown to have been imported; but it is possible to discern a Mediterranean influence in Scandinavian Bronze Age dress as a whole: for example, the girl's corded skirts, the man's cloak and knitted cap, the latter apparently intended for protection against excessive heat (Malmer 1970, p. 194).

A stone slab, which originally formed the gable end of a stone cist, and which is decorated with cupmarks and two ships of types AIa1 and CIa1 respectively (Althin 1945, Taf. 78 and Burenhult 1973, p. 64), was recovered from a barrow in Järrestad no. 4, Järrestad parish, Scania. The size of the cist (the length of a man) would suggest a date in the Early Bronze Age for these ship designs. The juxtaposition of two designs of different type and technique and a number of cup-marks suggests that this slab was not, like the Kivik stones, decorated when the grave was built, but that a stone was used which had had designs engraved upon it over a period of time.

On some rock-engravings the crew lines slant forward, as on the Rørby ship (fig. 4). An AIa1 ship on Simris no. 19, Scania, has crew lines which not only slant but are also grouped in pairs like those on the Rørby ship (Althin 1945, Taf. 7, bottom right and Taf. 11:1 in the foreground). It is the only ship on this site of type AIa1: the dominant types here are B and C. Ships of type C sometimes have slanting crew lines (Althin 1945, Taf. 5, left and Taf. 8, top right) and one ship of this type has crew lines which are grouped fairly regularly in pairs (Althin 1945, Taf. 5, far right). In Östergötland there are also some instances of forward slanting crew lines, mainly on type C ships (Nordén 1925 A, pl. 37, left and 77, centre). These details would suggest that ship designs of type C, and especially of type A, have a particularly close relationship to the Rørby ship, and must therefore have been fairly closely contemporary.

4.6.3. Type B and C ships

If the reason for the low frequency of type A ship designs in West Denmark (fig. 7) is due to the rapid replacement of this type by another (4.4.), we can only assume that type A was replaced by type B, which is the dominant type in this area. In this case it must be concluded that type B originated in West Denmark.

A date in the Early Bronze Age for type B is suggested by three ships of type BIIIa1 engraved on a roof slab of a megalithic tomb in Dilhøj, Grevinge parish, Sjælland (Glob 1969, fig. 9). The tomb was originally covered by a barrow in which a bronze dagger and some uncremated bones indicating an Early Bronze Age date were found during excavation in 1790 (Glob 1969, p. 49. Rostholm 1972, p. 7). If this find has

Fig. 14. The Sagaholm barrow: outer kerb of boulders and inner kerb of dressed sandstone slabs. (Photo: Anders Wihlborg.)

chronological significance it is important that the ships are of type BIIIa1. From this we may deduce that early type B ship designs ought to have crew lines (element a), but that they may have single prows (element III).

The only type C ship designs in West Denmark occur in the rock-engravings from Truehøjgård, Rold parish in Himmerland, Jutland. They occur on a small stone, barely 30 cm long, but comprise two ships, two naked feet, cup-marks and a representation of a man (Glob 1969, fig. 18:a–f). The stone was found during the investigation of a ploughed-out barrow, lying outside the remains of a stone frame which was possibly originally rectangular. The area enclosed by the frame was approximately 1×0.75 m (Glob 1969. fig. 227:a–b). According to Glob it could be the remains of a man-sized grave, and as cremated bones—or indeed uncremated bones and artefacts—were not found, he dates it to Period 2 or 3. (Glob 1969, pp. 49 and 232). But this need not have been a grave, for other structures (perhaps for cult purposes) are commonly found in Bronze Age barrows: and, if it was a grave it may have been of a different size. A better dating can be arrived at by a study of the foot designs on the stone (Glob 1969, fig. 18:e–f), for there are indications that designs of naked feet with toes belong to Period 4 (see below, 10.2). The small size of the stone from Truehøjgård suggests that all the figures were engraved at the same time, especially as they are all equally roughly drawn and cut. A date in Period 4 can therefore also be assigned to the ship designs.

A likely dating to the Early Bronze Age for type C ships is, however, indicated by the presence of two ship designs of types CIa1 and AIa1 on a stone from the man-sized cist in a barrow at Järrestad no. 4, Scania, discussed above (Althin 1945, Taf. 78, Burenhult 1973, p. 64). The distance between the stone cists at Järrestad and Kivik (4.6.2) is only 15 km. They must be considered together, and Period 3 is a reasonable date for both.

A date in the Early Bronze Age is also likely for the engravings in a barrow at Sagaholm, Ljungarum parish, Småland, which was investigated in 1971. The barrow lies within the confines of the area here called South-East Sweden, but, situated at the southern end of Lake Vättern, it is near the Östergötland border (Wihlborg 1978, fig. 1). The barrow, which was originally 22 m in diameter, and 3 m high, was damaged by sand quarrying so that at the time of the excavation only about the half of the periphery remained. The barrow was built of grass turf taken from sandy soil. There was an outer kerb of boulders and an inner kerb of dressed sandstone slabs, of which 45 were found in their original position. These stones are a little wider at the top than at the bottom and consequently lean slightly outwards (fig. 14). There are engravings on the outside faces of fifteen of the stones (two stones with similar decorations were found in a modern building, and presumably came from the damaged barrow). Among the motifs are seven ship designs, all of type C: two are type CIa1 (fig. 15:26), one of type CIb1 (fig. 15:6 top) and four of type CIc1 (fig. 15:6, bottom, 15:4 and 15:32).

The Sagaholm engravings should be treated as a closed find; thus all the engravings must have been executed at the time when the barrow was built. The figures are produced by pecking, although the prows are only incised and the hulls are smoothed (Wihlborg 1978, p. 125). In at least one instance the design is unfinished; the pecking of the hull does not extend over the whole surface (fig. 15:6 and Wihlborg 1978, Fig. 15).

C14 examination of charcoal found on the original land surface has produced a date of 3265 ± 130 BP, which assigns the Sagaholm barrow to the Early Bronze Age. Because of the damage to the barrow, no burial was found. However, another barrow in Ljungarum parish, has an identical kerb of dressed and outward-leaning slabs: the grave-goods in the central burial of this barrow are dated with certainty to Period 2. (Wihlborg 1978, p. 118).

A detail which suggests relative contemporaneity with the Kivik grave in the vertical line on the left side of one of the slabs at Sagaholm (fig. 15:6). This line can perhaps be compared with the frames on the Kivik stones (fig. 6), here interpreted as reflecting textile prototypes (4.6.2). In other respects there are no great real or formal similarities between

Sagaholm and Kivik and, while we know little or nothing about the burial cist at Sagaholm, we know equally little about a possible kerb round the Kivik grave (which was discovered as early as 1748). But the carefully dressed and richly decorated stone slabs of both structures have an important similarity, and they can both, without much doubt, be described as chieftains' graves.

The Sagaholm engravings can be dated with fair probability to Period 2 or 3 by means of the presumed date of the Kivik grave (Period 3), the evidence of the C14 date, and the similarity of construction between the Sagaholm grave and the other grave from Ljungarum (which is dated to Period 2). The combination of types CIa1, CIb1 and CIc1 at Sagaholm confirms the validity of the hypothesis, founded on a logical basis in the introduction of this chapter (4.2), that types CI, a1, b1 and c1 are nearly contemporary, and that they are earlier than CII–CIII, b2–b3 and c2–c3.

There are, therefore, indications that the Truehøjgård ship designs in West Denmark may be dated to Period 4, while the ship designs on the Järrestad cist in Skåne, and the Sagaholm stones in South-East Sweden, are from the Early Bronze Age.

Ship designs of type B and C are the result of small but striking changes in the design of type A: in the case of the former, one of the horizontals has been omitted, and in the case of the latter, the whole area of the hull is hammered out. From a technical and aesthetic point of view it is reasonable to suppose that the two changes (i.e. the creation of types B and C respectively) occured at about the same time.

It is most likely that ships of type B originated in West Denmark and type C in Scania. The types spread northwards in a somewhat retarded innovation pattern, the northern areas tending to continue in the production of type A ships. Type A ship designs originally spread northwards in an innovation pattern which, by comparison, was subject to little or no retardation (fig. 7–8).

The hypothesis that the innovation patterns of types B and C moved, as did type A, from south to north can be further reinforced by a study of variations in the geographical distribution of type A. In the whole of Northern Europe, 78.5 % of element A (double-line ships) is combined with element I (ships with two double prows), 8 % with element II (ships with one double and one single prow) and 13.5 % with element III (ships with two single prows). But the proportions of AI designs show a characteristic geographical variation: in West Denmark the share of type AI is 100 %, whilst in Scania it is 95 % and in Östergötland 85 %. Thus the combination AI, which we know to be of early origin because of the Rørby sword design of type AIa1, becomes successively *less common* from south to north, although the proportion of type A ships rises from south to north (fig. 8–9). On the other hand the combinations AII and AIII become *more common* from south to north: the proportion of type

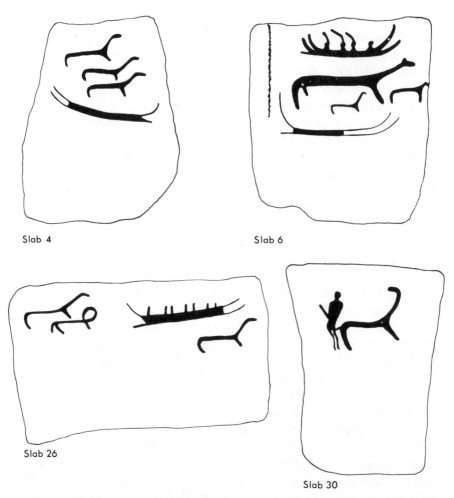

Fig. 15 a. Decorated stone slabs from the Sagaholm barrow. (After Wihlborg 1978.)

AII designs in West Denmark is 0 %, in Scania 5 % and in Östergötland 11 %, while the figures for type AIII designs are West Denmark and Scania 0 % and Östergötland 4 %.

The western diffusion route shows a similar pattern: the proportion of type AI designs in Denmark is 100 %, in Bohuslän 91 % and in Rogaland 75.5 %; consequently type AI becomes successively *less common* from south to north, although the proportion of type A ships rises from south to north (fig. 7). But type AII becomes *more common* in areas to the north: the figure from West Denmark is 0 %, for Bohuslän 7.5 % and for Rogaland 15.5 %. The equivalent figures for type AIII are: West Denmark 0 %, Bohuslän 1.5 % and Rogaland 9 %. These figures can only be interpreted in one way: the prow designs II and III are of later origin than I, which is found on the Rørby sword. The gradual increase in the

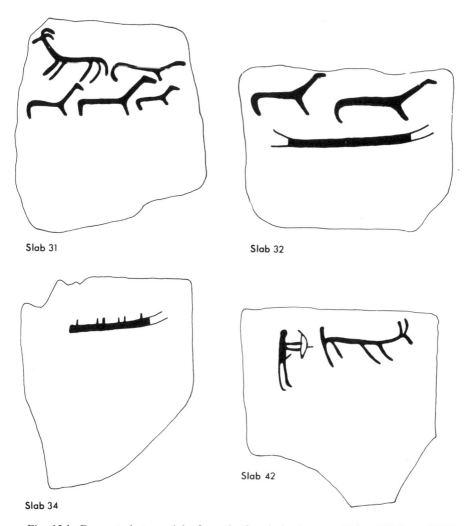

Slab 31

Slab 32

Slab 34

Slab 42

Fig. 15 b. Decorated stone slabs from the Sagaholm barrow. (After Wihlborg 1978.).

proportion of types AII and AIII towards the north is related to the fact that types B and C, which developed in southern Scandinavia (probably in West Denmark and Scania respectively), were only adopted in areas to the north after considerable delay, resulting in a greater production of the later type A designs (AII and AIII) in northern areas.

4.6.4. Type D and E ships

The contoured D ships are a phenomenon of the western areas. They occur mainly in Trøndelag and Rogaland, in which two areas are found 58 of the 81 type D ships in the original corpus. The remaining 23 are distributed in eight areas, of which four are also in the west (table 2).

Type E ship designs, which have more than two horizontal lines on the hull, also show a bias towards a western distribution, especially in Rogaland, which posesses 27 of the 66 type E ships in the original corpus. The remaining designs of this type are distributed over almost the entire area in which the ship motif occurs: 24, however, come from West Sweden, Bohuslän, Østfold, South Norway, Middle Norway and Trøndelag.

Contoured ships (type D) occur, despite their small numbers (equivalent to one tenth of type C ships, one fifteenth of type B ships and one twentieth of type A ships), on an unusually large number of datable bronze objects. Thus, for instance, on the well-known razor from Viemose, Kallehave parish on south-west Sjælland (Broholm 1946, pp. 33–34, Grave 266. Glob 1969, p. 53 and fig. 33) which is usually dated to Period 4, there is a design which is surprisingly similar to those found in rock-engravings, and can easily be classified as type DIa2. A ship design on a razor with a square handle from Fælledskoven, Dråby parish, Sjælland (Glob 1969, p. 53, fig. 36) may clearly be classified as type DIc1. Such razors are firmly dated to Period 5, and it is thus clear that type D ship designs were still produced during that period.

The apparent paradox of the rare type D ship design being particularly easily datable by reference to examples engraved on bronze objects is easily explained in that contoured designs are especially suited to the techniques of bronze engraving. It is indeed possible to suggest that the type D ship design was created not as a motif for rock-engraving, but to suit the particular techniques of engraving on metal. The curiously random distribution of type D rock-engravings in many areas may be explained if such designs spread partly or entirely by means of engraved razors, which were produced in West Denmark and copied on rock surfaces throughout Northern Europe.

No type E ships occur in closed finds, and there are no designs of this type engraved on bronze. But the designs on bronze may perhaps provide a clue, in that large numbers of parallel horizontal lines are typical of ship designs on bronze of the Late Bronze Age (Glob 1969, p. 53, figs. 34–36). It is possible to regard type E ships of rock art as coarse and misunderstood versions of the multiple line ship design found on metal. A connection between type E and type D, which are obviously influenced by bronze engraving, is suggested by the fact that both types are concentrated in Norway. Norway's share of all rock-engravings of ships is only 33 %, but its share of type E ships is no less than 66 %, and of type D ships 78 %. No area has a greater total of type D and E ships than Rogaland.

The most likely date for type E ships is therefore the Late Bronze Age, the type having perhaps evolved in Period 4 at the same time as the type D ship design.

4.7. Ship designs at Nämforsen

North of the Mälar region in Sweden, ship designs are only found at Nämforsen in Ångermanland. In his excellent publication of 1960, Hallström lists 366 boat or ship designs, of which 342 are described as completely certain (Hallström 1960, p. 293). Table 6 lists only 220 ships, comprising those which the author could classify with reference to the four groups of elements which define the types.

Hallström states that only a few boat and ship figures at Nämforsen are of Bronze Age character, and he classifies the rest as of 'Nämforsen type' (Hallström 1960, pp. 295–296). However, all the ship designs at Nämforsen are easily fitted into the system of classification used in this study.

The Nämforsen engravings are divided topographically in table 6 according to Hallström's divisions: Nämforsen II comprises Notön in the east, Nämforsen III the central Brådön, and Nämforsen I both banks of Ångermanälven, including Laxön: this island was created recently by blasting a channel, and was part of the north bank of the river in prehistoric times (see map fig. 26).

Animal figures dominate the site and are fairly evenly distributed between the areas Nämforsen I–III (table 28). The ship designs, on the contrary, are unevenly distributed, with Brådön (Nämforsen III) having the fewest examples. The ship types are also unequally distributed, type A designs representing 92 % on the islands (Nämforsen II–III), but only 69 % on the river banks (Nämforsen I). It is also apparent that the islands have early examples like types AI and AII, while Nämforsen I (the river banks) has only type AIII. Notön (Nämforsen II) has one example of the hypothetical prototype AIa1 (Hallström 1960, pl. 18:G:1). The central Brådön (Nämforsen III) has 6 AI and AII ships, as against 7 type AIII ships. The ships of types AIa2, AIc2, AIIa1 and AIIa2 from Brådön (Hallström 1960, pl. 25:E:4–6 and 26:Q:2) serve to increase the probability that the classification to AIa1 of the damaged design from Nämforsen II is correct. All these factors seem to justify the hypothesis that the engravings of ship designs at Nämforsen started on the islands (II and III) and later spread to the river banks (I).

The commonest ship type at Nämforsen is AIIIc1, which alone accounts for 46 % of all ship designs. It is a double-line ship without crew or ribs and with two single prows, usually with an animal head (presumably an elk) at the stem (Hallström 1960, pl. 10:A:9, bottom). The next most common types are AIIIa1 (the same ship with crew lines—Hallström 1960, pl. 14:G:6), AIIIa2 (the same ship with crew lines and rib lines—Hallström 1960, pl. 18:E:2, bottom right) and AIIIc2 (the same ship with rib lines but no crew—Hallström 1960, pl. 21:S:5). Those ships which have crew or ribs (AIIIa1, AIIIa2 and AIIIc2) seems to be better executed than the large body of ships without either crew or ribs (AIIIc1). The former are more like the South Scandinavian prototype (AIa1) and this may be taken as an indication that the 'Nämforsen type' has a direct association with the South Scandinavian ship type. The ship motif is not generally used in European rock art; it has a special association with South Scandinavian farming rock-engravings and North Scandinavian hunting rock-engravings. Initially, therefore, it seems less likely that the two groups of ship designs should be unconnected (cf. Bakka 1975, pp. 119–121).

At Nämforsen there are 30 type B ships (single-line ships—Hallström 1960, pl. 13), which represent 13.5 % of all ship designs. 20 of these are from the river banks (Nämforsen I), which may suggest that type B ships at Nämforsen are later than ships of type A.

The three examples of type C ship designs (Hallström 1960, pl. 18:E:1–2) all come from Notön (Nämforsen II).

It is possible that there is a connection between the Karelian ships of types B and C, which have stems decorated with animal heads (Hallström 1960, Pl. 28) and the Nämforsen ships. However, there are no certainly identified rock-engravings in North Finland; in South Finland there are rock-paintings but no engravings. Ship designs from only one site in South Finland, Astuvansalmi, Savolaks, are included in the original corpus (table 1–3), but ship designs from two other sites in Savolaks have recently been published (Sarvas and Taavitsainen 1976).

The rock-paintings are necessarily coarser and show less detail than the engravings, but it seems obvious that the Finnish paintings should be considered together with the South Scandinavian ship designs, especially as one of the ships from Astuvansalmi is combined with a circular design (Sarvas 1969, p. 19, Abb. 17). Among the recently discovered paintings from Savolaks is a ship of type CIIa1; here the whole hull has been painted in, and it has an animal head on the prow at the stem (Sarvas and Taavitsainen 1976, p. 38, Kuva 12). This seems, therefore, to provide a link both with the type C ships of eastern Scandinavia and with Nämforsen.

5. Carts

5.1. Terminology and classification

The elements of cart representations which can be identified with most certainty are the presence or absence of draught animals and driver, and the number and design of the wheels (fig. 16). The following definitions may be formulated:

A   Cart with draught animals and driver.
B   Cart with draught animals but no driver.
C   Cart without draught animals or driver.
1   Two-wheeled cart.
2   Four-wheeled cart.
3   Cart depicted with only one wheel.
a   Wheel with four spokes.
b   Wheel depicted as a circle with a central dot or as two concentric circles.
c   Wheel depicted as an empty circle.
d   Wheel depicted as a filled circle (the whole surface is hammered-out).

Type definitions produced by combining one element from each of these three groups of symbols represent mutually exclusive types.

5.2. Chorology and chronology

The typological elements defined above (5.1) make up a classification system with a capacity of 36 types. The original corpus consists of 61 cart designs (table 7).

It was earlier postulated that the ship motif first appeared in West Denmark, and that it spread northwards in such a manner that three diffusion routes can be identified. This hypothesis must be considered with regard to the distribution of cart designs, but it is important to point out that in Denmark this motif has not so far been found on engravings on rocks or in graves. The area where cart designs occur most frequently is Bohuslän, which alone has 28 examples, almost half the total number. Next are Scania with 16 and Østfold with 13 cart designs; South-East Sweden, Östergötland and West Sweden each have only one or two of these designs. The general picture, therefore, suggests that the cart representations belong to the area immediately to the east of West Denmark: Scania, West Sweden, Bohuslän and Østfold together possess 58 of the 61 cart designs of the corpus.

Table 7 shows the number of ship designs in each area, and the number of cart designs expressed as a percentage of the number of ships. In the whole of Northern Europe there are 61 cart designs and 3877 ship designs; thus the carts amount to 1.5 % of the ships. With 14.5 % Scania has by far the largest proportion of carts in relation to ship designs. The next largest is found in Østfold, where it is only 4 %.

Thus carts are much rarer than ships, and this has consequences for any attempt at interpretation. We may postulate that the ship was a more universal symbol, perhaps an apotropaic symbol known throughout Northern Europe, serving to ward off evil (Malmer 1970, p. 199). The cart designs, on the other hand, might allude to a specific cult ceremony. It is possible that this ceremony, a ritual processon of carts, was actually performed in Denmark with real carts, draught animals and drivers—or else with bronze models of the Trundholm cart type—and that for this reason no engraved designs of carts occur here. In the areas immediately to the east of Denmark, in Scania-Bohuslän-Østfold, actual cart rituals may have been replaced by rock-engravings. And we may finally propose that in areas further removed from Denmark, cart rituals were less well known, and were consequently rarely or never depicted in rock art.

The distribution of the separate elements and types differs considerably in the geographical areas. Element A (cart with draught animals and driver) is rare; two of a total of five examples come from Scania: the two well-known engravings found on stone no. 7 in the Kivik grave (fig. 6:7 and 16:1) and the Villfara stone (Althin 1945, Taf. 81). Both are of type A1a, which indicates that they have two four-spoked wheels as well as draught animals and driver. Type A1a presumably represents the earliest type of cart design; first because it occurs in the Kivik grave, which is dated to Period 3 (discussed above in 4.6.2), and secondly because of the unambiguous realism of the engravings, and their obvious association with Mediterranean—and specifically Mycenean—types (Marstrander 1963, pp. 176–200). Another two cart designs can—with some hesitation—be assigned to type A1a: both are from Östergötland, from Fiskeby and Herrebro (Nordén 1925 A, pl. 92 and 122). In the case of the former engraving the driver is not clearly seen on available illustrations, while on the latter the driver is clearly represented but the wheels are ill-defined. It is quite clear, however, that they should both be grouped with type A1a. This provides confirmation of the rapid communications between Scania and Östergötland in the Early Bronze Age also indicated, for instance, by the presence in Östergötland of ship designs with slanting crew-lines.

Apart from the two designs of type A1a, the remaining 14 cart designs from Scania have two four-spoked wheels and no drivers; an equal number are shown with draught animals (type B1a) and without (C1a). The design is clear and obviously represents a chariot of the same general type as that from Kivik, although it is seen from a slightly different angle.

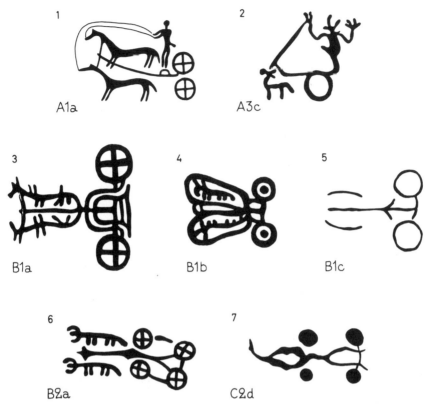

Fig. 16. Cart designs.
(Sites: *1:* Kivik, Scania. *2:* Vitlycke, Bohuslän. *3:* Frännarp, Scania. *4:* Disåsen, Bohuslän. *5:* Begby, Østfold. *6:* Rished, Bohuslän. *7:* Solberg, Østfold.)

It would seem to be significant that all the cart designs from Scania, as well as the two carts from Östergötland of type A1a, have four-spoked wheels (element a). Table 7 shows a different situation in Bohuslän where wheel types b and d dominate, and in Østfold, where only one of 13 cart designs has four-spoked wheels. Designs with type c and d wheels (represented by empty and filled circles respectively) are often clearly a simplified form of cart designs with type a wheels (fig. 16:5 and 7). These facts all point to the same conclusion: the engraving of cart designs started a little later in Bohuslän than in Scania, but the practice continued for a considerably longer period in Bohuslän and Østfold.

Four-wheeled carts (element 2) only occur in Bohuslän (seven examples) and Østfold (six examples). In the design of draught animals and wheels they are sometimes similar to the early two-wheeled carts (fig. 16:6), but they are frequently much simplified (fig. 16:7). Thus the date of these carts can presumably be placed a little later than that of the two-wheeled carts.

It is interesting to speculate on the origin of the design of the four-wheeled cart. One plausible explanation is that the four-wheeled type is an adaptation of the design of the carts actually in use in Bohuslän and Østfold. If this hypothesis is accepted, it is also necessary to postulate that ship designs—while on the one hand developing into baroque and fantastic forms—also developed more realistic features by imitating the design of real Nordic ships; an argument which Marstrander in particular has maintained, supported by much circumstantial argument (Marstrander 1963, pp. 79–166).

It is unlikely that two-wheeled chariots actually existed in Bohuslän and Østfold in the Bronze Age. The realism of the design of the chariot in the Kivik grave is astounding (fig. 16:1), but this may perhaps be explained as having been copied from an imported Mediterranean picture, perhaps on a textile (4.6.2). The presence of carts in Denmark in the Early Bronze Age is best demonstrated by the Trundholm find, but any speculation as to whether the carts—which according to our hypothesis were used in the cult in Denmark—were in any way similar to the Kivik and Villfara carts will not be discussed here.

5.3. Additional material

Ten cart designs, mainly taken from recent literature, have been registered in addition to those listed in table 7.

From the Scania site of Frännarp, Gryt parish, seven carts of type B1a and five of type C1a (i.e. with and without draught animals respectively) can be distinguished in Althin 1945, Taf, 73. Burenhult 1973, pp. 62–63, illustrates a further three carts of type C1a.

Three additional designs are taken from Bohuslän, the other principal area of cart designs: one of type B1c in Svenneby, and two of types C2b and A1a from Bottna (Fredsjö et al. 1971, pl. 47, and 1975, pls. 65 and 69). The suggested prototype A1a therefore also occurs in Bohuslän, with the reservation that the spokes of the wheels are recorded as unclear. By comparison with the Kivik chariot the drawing is considerably simplified.

In peripheral areas cart designs have also been noted. In Uppland there are three carts of types A1c, B2b and B3b. (Kjellén 1939, p. 92, fig. 11. Kjellén-Hyenstrand 1976, p. 123, fig. 2 and p. 142, Fig. 40). The most remote example is a cart design of type A1c in Askvoll, Sogn og Fjordane, Middle Norway (Bakka 1971, p. 2).

The additional material does not justify any alteration of the hypotheses presented in 5.2. The relative proportions in the geographical areas remain essentially unchanged.

6. Ards

In the preceeding section, some support was found for a tentative hypothesis to the effect that rock-engravings portraying cult scenes are particularly common in the areas immediately to the east of West Denmark, from Skåne in the south to Østfold in the north. The establishment of this hypothesis is to some extent further justified by the evidence of representations of ploughing. All engravings with this motif (of which the author knows eight) are found in Bohuslän, distributed among seven sites (Glob 1951, pp. 25, 45, 54).

It cannot, of course, be maintained that ploughing—whether for practical or ritual purposes—was either unknown or unusual in Bohuslän. Neither, however, can it be claimed that the distribution of ploughing scenes in rock art could significantly reflect the extent of agriculture in the Bronze Age. Today agricultural land in Bohuslän represents 18 % of the whole area, while in Denmark the figure is 65 %, and there is no reason to believe that Bohuslän was relatively more important as an agricultural area in the Bronze Age. It is perhaps even possible that the interest in ploughing scenes in Bohuslän was stimulated by the fact that the prevailing conditions for agriculture left a lot to be desired.

It is, however, possible to theorise further concerning the origin of the ploughing motif. Ard designs occur in the parishes of Brastad, Tossene and Tanum. All three parishes also possess representations of carts, and Tanum has the largest number both of carts and ards. Three engravings depict both carts and ards, those from Backa in Brastad, and from Finntorp and Aspeberget in Tanum; in one part of the Backa engravings the relationship is even closer, in that within a group of six carts is an ard pulled (as in most representations of ploughing) by two horned draught animals (Baltzer 1881–1890, pl. 6). As with three of the cart designs nearby, the feet of both draught animals are turned towards the beam. It is therefore possible to postulate that the ploughing scenes developed from representations of carts, just as designs depicting four-wheeled carts developed from two-wheeled carts in an attempt to adapt the engraved designs to the designs of carts then used in Bohuslän. Thus the two-wheeled chariots, which bore no relation to practical usage in the area, were replaced by ards and four-wheeled carts.

According to Glob's investigations the engravings portray ploughing implements of differing construction: crook ards (fig. 17:1), bow ards (fig. 17:2) and stave ards (fig. 17:3). It can be seen, therefore, that this motif is treated more realistically than most of those found in rock art;

Fig. 17. Ard designs.
(Sites (all in Tanum, Bohuslän): *1:* Litsleby. *2:* Aspeberget. *3:* Finntorp.)

the realism of the Bohuslän engravings and the prevalence of scenes in this area are naturally connected.

The ard is in most cases pulled by two oxen and guided by a ploughman. In one instance the ploughman is phallic (fig. 17:1), and on one engraving the ard is pulled by only one animal (Glob 1951, p. 55, figs. 61–62). On yet another figure there are two horned, draught animals, but no ploughman behind the ard (Baltzer 1881–1890, pl.55:4). One ard is represented without either draught animal or ploughman; but it would seem rash to interpret this design differently from the others, i.e. as a sacrifice (Almgren 1964, pp. 155–158 and fig. 4).

The only possible means of dating ploughing scenes would seem to be through their association with cart designs. The Kivik cart enables us to assign them to Period 3 or, presumably, to subsequent periods.

7. Weapons

7.1. Terminology and classification

In rock art, weapons are depicted to various scales—at natural size, and both larger and smaller than natural size. While there are obvious practical reasons why representations of ships, carts and ards are always portrayed at a reduced size, it is worth considering whether the different scales to which the weapons were portrayed did not serve a significant purpose, as has been suggested, notably by Almgren (1962, pp. 63–66).

The weapons are depicted either with or without hafts, and sometimes carried by men, either at the side or raised in the hand. They may be represented at natural size, enlarged, or in miniature.

Thus we have:

1 Unhafted weapons. Always of natural, or slightly greater than natural, size.
2 Hafted weapons, not carried. Always of natural, or slightly greater than natural size.
3 Hafted weapons, carried:
   a Weapon of natural, or slightly greater than natural, size, and the man in miniature.
   b Both weapon and man of natural, or slightly greater than natural, size.
   c Both weapon and man in miniature.

It would seem that the common group 3:c may be contrasted with groups 1,2 and 3:a. In the latter groups the weapons are emphasized, whilst in group 3:c, although the weapon is obviously important, attention is drawn to the design as a whole, i.e. primarily to the man (or god). It seems reasonable to consider group 3:b together with group 3:c, since the large size of the design in relation to the surrounding engravings focuses the main attention of the whole figure of the man (or god).

In this chapter only groups 1, 2 and 3:a will be considered, because in these the main emphasis is on the weapon. Groups 3:b and 3:c will be considered together with other representations of the human figure (see chapter 12).

To avoid unnecessary detail and the risk of exceeding the framework of the present study, the following definitions will suffice:

A   Axe (fig. 18:1–2).
D   Dagger or sword (fig. 18:5).
S   Spear (fig. 18:3–4).

C   Ceremonial weapons: axes formed by a convex upper line and a concave lower line; the convex line not being broken by projections (fig. 18:8).

E   Elk-headed axes: axes with a head formed by a convex upper line and a concave lower line; one or two projections are added to the convex line at the end of the head nearest the haft. Hafted naturalistic representations of elk heads also belongs to this group (fig. 18:6–7).

1   Unhafted (fig. 6:6).

2   Hafted but not carried (fig. 18:1, 3, 6, 8).

3   Hafted and carried (fig. 18:2, 4, 7).

7.2. Chorology and chronology

The distribution of the 457 classified weapon designs in the original corpus is shown in table 8. As was the case with carts and ards, the distribution is irregular. A comparison with these groups does, however, reveal striking differences: the most important areas for cart designs are Scania, Bohuslän and Østfold, while the areas with the largest number of sword, spear and axe designs are Scania, Östergötland and the Mälar District. The distribution of cart and weapon designs is therefore similar in that both are numerous in Scania and absent in Denmark. However, the cart designs are found predominantly in western areas, while weapon designs are more common in the east. The difference seems significant: the cart designs may be interpreted as alluding to ritual ceremonies, whereas the axe designs may be seen as allusions to the sacrifice of axes. If so, South Scandinavia can be divided into three areas. In West Denmark—the central area—neither cart ceremonies nor axe offerings were depicted, which may be explained hypothetically by postulating that such activities were actually practised in this region. In those western areas of the Scandinavian peninsula closest to Denmark, engraved carts occur, hypothetically because ceremonies involving carts were known, but not practised. In the eastern areas of the Scandinavian peninsula (including Scania) engravings of weapon designs occur, which may be explained by postulating that sacrifices of weapons were known, but practised less frequently than in Denmark; in this area, however, no cart designs occur on rock-engravings, presumably because ceremonies involving carts were not sufficiently well-known (save in Scania) to attract the interest of the rock artist.

The last column of table 8 shows the ratio (expressed as a percentage) of weapon designs to ship designs. This figure is a more reliable guide than plain numbers in considering the interest in representations of weapons in the various areas. But the figures must of course be used with some caution. Of 86 weapon designs in Scania, no less than 60 come from a single site, Simris no 19. A marked preference for a certain design can naturally depend on quite irrelevant circumstances, as for instance the personal tastes or interests of the individual artist. On the other hand, the

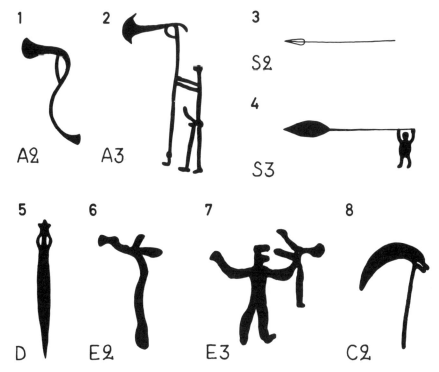

Fig. 18. Weapon designs.
(Sites: *1:* Himmelstalund, Östergötland. *2:* Simris nr 19, Scania. *3:* Tuna in Bälinge, Uppland, Mälar District. *4:* Leonardsberg, Östergötland. *5:* Fiskeby, Östergötland. *6:* Nämforsen, Ångermanland. *7:* Nämforsen, Ångermanland. *8:* Vingen in Nordfjord, Middle Norway.)

fact that weapon designs occur on six different sites in Scania reflects a significant interest in this motif. The significance of such numbers can best be confirmed if similar values are found in considering a range of types. An important trend has already been observed on several occasions, whereby the southern central areas—West Denmark and Scania—have low percentages of ship designs, whereas the proportions of other types of design are very high. Thus the variety of rock art subjects in the southern central areas is in some respects greater than in the northern areas. It is more commonly said that the images in the rock art of Östergötland–Bohuslän–Østfold are far richer than in Denmark-Scania. Also this opinion is to an extent justified. There are far greater quantities of rock art in the northern regions, and it is thus more likely that unusual variants will occur; equally, the engravings are characterised by the northern artist's superior ability to portray the human figure in a greater variety of ways, thus creating a much livelier impression.

The variety of weapon designs differs considerably from one area to another. Unhafted axe designs (A1) occur only in Scania, at the top of stone no 6 in the Kivik grave (fig. 6:6). This type of design is therefore known to have occurred in Period 3, but unhafted weapon designs are among the earliest motifs of the Bronze Age, and are found engraved on bronze as early as the transition period 1/2 on the Fårdrup axes and on a flanged flat-axe (Malmer 1970, pp. 190–195). Most of the weapon designs in Scandia portray axes of the Early Bronze Age (and probably flanged axes in particular) as, for example, the majority of axe designs at Simris no 19. There is no reason to believe that any axe design in Scania belongs to the Late Bronze Age.

In Östergötland axe designs still outnumber spear designs, which do not occur in Scania. In the Mälar District, however, there are more representations of spears than of axes, and in Bohuslän the few weapon designs which exist all portray spears.

It is difficult to date the spear designs. Spear-bearers are found on the Wismar trumpet from Period 3 (fig. 5), but they carry round shields and are very small in size; it is thus very questionable if they can be associated with the spear-bearers found in Östergötland and Bohuslän. But men carrying spears, whether those of the Wismar trumpet or of rock-engravings, are usually not phallic, whereas men carrying axes invariably are; this is true for the motifs considered in this chapter as well as those where the men and the axes they carry are represented to the same scale. The difference between axe and spear was therefore not solely one of form and function; they also belonged to different mythological and ritual spheres.

Daggers and swords occur only in Östergötland; they are never carried. Hilts and blades refer them to Period 2–3.

Both at Nämforsen (Ångermanland) and Vingen (Middle Norway) animal-headed weapons play an important role. It is difficult to construct a chronology based on the material available so far. It is attractive to imagine a typological-chronological series, beginning with naturalistic animal-headed axes, continuing through bommerang-shaped axes with ears to end with those without ears. But there are many other possibilities. Those naturalistic elk-headed axes which are carried can be compared with axes which are carried at Simris; this may possibly be interpreted as an indication of a date in the Early Bronze Age (Moberg 1970, p. 226).

7.3. Additional material

Examination of publications from 1972–79 (3.1) has not produced any material which alters in any significant manner the results obtained from the original corpus. It is particularly noticeable that the major publications of material from Kville, Bohuslän, and Hordaland, Middle Norway, have produced no weapon designs. Our conclusion, therefore, remains unchanged: the interest in weapon designs of the South Scandinavian Bronze Age type is focused on Scania and the eastern areas of Sweden.

8. Clothing

Bertil Almgren (1960, p. 19) has convincingly interpreted as cloaks a
number of designs, usually kidney-shaped and about two metres in length
(fig. 19:1), and as tunics two rectangular designs from Uppland with two
extended corners corresponding to shoulder straps (fig. 19:2). Two designs, also from Uppland, shaped like a segment of a circle and just over
three metres long (fig. 19:3), may represent a bigger type of cloak, folded
in two.

A chorological corpus of only ten figures has naturally only a limited
weight. Table 9, however, at least suggests that representations of clothing have an easterly distribution, being concentrated in Scania, Östergötland and in particular in the Mälar District. In the west, clothing designs
occur only at one site in Bohuslän (Nasseröd, Svenneby parish—Fredsjö
et al. 1971, p. 12), where three kidney-shaped cloak designs are engraved
in close proximity to each other. Thus six sites in east Sweden have
clothing designs, but only one site in west Sweden.

The easterly distribution of clothing designs conforms to the distribution of weapon designs, and differs from the designs of carts and ards,
which have a westerly distribution. Clothing designs also share a formal
similarity with weapon designs in that both are represented at approximately natural size, whereas the ceremonial designs in the west are
depicted in miniature. This trend serves to strengthen the hypothesis that
there is a contrast between sacrificial designs in the east and ceremonial
designs in the west.

The small number of engravings of clothing suggests that such designs
were not produced for any length of time. If we see weapon and clothing
designs as expressions of the same custom—and this seems undeni-
able—then they should be contemporary. The kidney-shaped cloak designs can be assigned to Period 2–3, while the segmental cloak designs
and the designs of tunics may be slightly later.

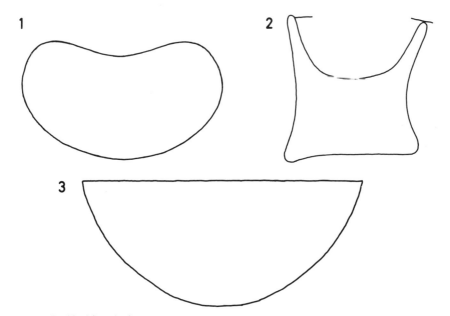

Fig. 19. Clothing designs.
1: Kidney-shaped cloak (Norrköpings Egna Hem, Östergötland). *2:* Tunic (Rickeby, Boglösa, Uppland, Mälar District). *3:* Cloak, shaped like the segment of a circle (Yttergånsta, Vårfrukyrka, Uppland, Mälar District).

9. Hands

Table 10 shows the distribution of a total of 33 hand designs, including those from recent publications (Capelle 1972, p. 233. Mandt 1972, pl. 41. Rostholm 1972, p. 2). The motif has a pronounced westerly distribution. Apart from West Denmark, where two-thirds of the material is found, hand designs occur in North Germany, Bohuslän and Norway.

The ratio of hand designs to ship designs in West Denmark is 73 %. In the rest of Northern Europe the ratio of hand designs to ship designs is less than 1 %. In West Denmark there was no impulsion to represent either ceremonies or sacrifices in rock-engravings, because, according to our hypothesis, such activities were actually performed there. On the other hand, it was apparently popular to engrave apotropaic symbols, also in burials.

Two types of hand design can be distinguished: in one the hand is shown with part of the forearm (fig. 20:1), in some cases depicting the whole forearm, with the elbow and a portion of the upper arm (fig. 20:2); in the other type, the hand only is depicted (Capelle 1972, Abb. 9). The thumb is usually well separated from the other fingers, especially in designs of the first type, which include portions of the arm. The type which depicts the hand alone is usually only found on outcrops of rock, while the type with hand and arm occurs only on loose slabs, most of which can be shown to have come from burial cists.

Table 10 shows a significant difference between the distribution patterns of the two types. The hand-and-arm motif occurs mainly in West Denmark and otherwise only in Østfold. But the less common type, depicting the hand alone, has a wider distribution, from North Germany in the south to Trøndelag in the north.

The interpretation of the hand design as an apotropaic symbol is suggested by the bronze figures from Grevensvænge, Sjælland. Both figures, that of a man, which is preserved, as well as the now lost figure of a woman, hold one hand pressed against the chest with the thumb pointing upwards (Broholm 1952 A, fig. 8–10. Broholm 1953, figs. 105 and 319). This gesture appears to suggest neither blessing, invocation or command, but rather a sign to bring luck or ward off evil. Brooches with a hand design on the back should also be considered in this context (Malmer 1970, p. 193, fig. 3:2). The wearer of a brooch with this design on the back would be constantly protected by a gesture which supposedly served to avert evil. The fact that the sign would not be seen

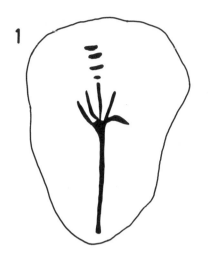

Fig. 20. Hand designs.
(Sites: *1:* Rævebakke, Sjælland, West Denmark. 2: Vestre Løkke, Østfold.)

when the brooch was worn supports the hypothesis of its apotropaic nature.

The four lines often seen beyond the fingertips of the hand-and-arm designs (fig. 20) can be interpreted as reinforcing its apotropaic properties. There are four lines in no less than twelve examples, whereas five or six lines each occur only once. Clearly one of the central concepts of Bronze Age thought concerned the figure two, and its property of doubling and redoubling. The idea behind this design could therefore perhaps be expressed thus: twice times double protection. The occasional presence of five or six lines signifies perhaps that the original concept was no longer properly understood by the artist.

The fact that the hand motif is found in burials makes it unusually easy to date, and the following finds provide the best dating evidence. The roof slab of a small cist in Lille Havelse, Sjælland, has three hand-and-arm designs, of which one, and probably two, had four lines beyond the fingertips. The cist contained burnt bones, a ring and a bronze stud, which positively dates it to Period 4. A wall slab from another small cist from Galgebakke, Slots Bjergby, Sjælland, is also decorated with three hand-and-arm designs, between which are a number of lines, apparently five. The grave contained a tweezer, razor and knife, which date the burial to Period 4 (Glob 1969, p. 206, no. 5 and p. 219, no. 41).

A find from Bunsoh, Schleswig-Holstein, may be of a different date. A number of engraved designs were found on one of the three roof slabs of a neolithic chamber tomb. These included at least one pair of hands (without arms) and the representation of a naked foot. It is stated that an Early Bronze Age burial lay over the roof slabs (Capelle 1972, p. 234) and it is therefore possible (although hardly conclusively documented) that these North German hand designs are older than the Danish hand-and-arm designs of Period 4.

Brooches bearing the hand motif on their backs do not belong to Period 4, but to Period 5 (five examples from Scania and one each from West Denmark, West Sweden and South Norway) or to Period 6 (seven examples from South-East Sweden and two from the Mälar District).

The chronology and innovation pattern of the hand motif can therefore be outlined thus: it originates in North Germany, perhaps already in the Early Bronze Age (Period 3?), and is found in the typical form of a hand-and-arm design with four lines in West Denmark in Period 4. During Periods 4 and 5, bronze figures also occur in West Denmark and Scania, which display an ostentatious hand gesture, the thumb separated from the fingers. In Period 5 the hand motif is found on brooches in West Denmark, Scania and western areas of the Scandinavian peninsula. Finally, in Period 6 the hand motif also appears on brooches in the eastern areas of the Scandinavian peninsula, from South-East Sweden to the Mälar District.

10. Feet

10.1. Terminology and classification

Representations of feet have a small number of easily identified typological elements. Feet are either drawn in outline, *contoured*, or the whole surface is *hammered-out*. They can be depicted with or without *toes*. Sometimes one or more lines cross the longitudinal axis at right angles, bisecting the design approximately in the middle (i.e. at the "instep"); this feature will be called a *cross strap*. Finally, feet may occur either *singly* or *in pairs*. The last element can usually be determined objectively without any difficulty if, that is, a foot design occurs by itself or if it is one of a pair. But there are some instances, especially on sites where there are many foot designs, when a margin of error must be accepted.

The eight typological elements are defined as follows:

A   With toes.
B   Without toes.
I   Single.
II   In pairs.
a   Without cross strap.
b   With cross strap.
1   Hammered-out.
2   Contoured.

10.2. Chorology and chronology

Foot designs are common. 1016 were classified from the basic literature, each design being reckoned as a separate figure regardless of whether or not it is one of a pair. If a pair of foot designs is counted as one figure, the number is reduced to 738, comprising 460 single foot designs and 278 pairs. Of sixteen theoretically possible types all are represented in the material, save AIb1 and AIIb1 (table 11).

Type AIa1 (fig. 21:1) can hardly be interpreted as anything but a realistic portrayal of a footprint (the imprint, for example, of a naked, wet foot on a smooth rock surface). By analogy with this interpretation, designs such as those illustrated in fig. 21:11–12 can fairly be seen as impressions of feet wearing some kind of footwear. They may, for the sake of convenience, be called *shoe designs* (although no real shoes are known from the Bronze Age), and this name can be applied to all designs of type B. Analogously, all type A designs are called *naked feet*. Types AIb2 (fig. 21:3) and AIIb2, that is naked feet with a cross strap at the instep, are so rare (there are three single feet and one pair, see table 11) that it is hardly worth discussing whether they are intended to portray naked feet with some kind of strap under the instep. It may also simply be a case of a typological contamination by Aa and Bb foot designs.

Tables 11 and 12 show that type B feet (shoe designs) are considerably more common than type A feet (naked feet). Foot designs are most common in Östergötland, followed by Scania, West Sweden, Bohuslän and Rogaland. But since actual numbers can be influenced by the efficiency of listing and publication, it is probably more accurate to express the frequency of foot designs as a percentage of the number of ship designs (as in the last column of table 12). In this relative sequence of foot designs, West Sweden leads with 336 % (showing that there are more than three times as many foot designs as ship designs), followed by Scania with 135 % and West Denmark with 96 %. The foot designs therefore show a marked south-westerly distribution, with a concentration in West Denmark and the adjoining areas to the east. It is striking that foot designs play a relatively minor role in the adjacent and very rich areas of Bohuslän and Østfold (here they have the low values of 11.5 % and 5.5 %).

The chorological relationship between the naked foot design (type A) and the shoe design (type B) is best illustrated by table 13. Type B feet occur in all areas except Finland-Karelia; whereas type A feet have a marked south-westerly distribution, occuring in Denmark, Bohuslän, Østfold, South Norway, Rogaland, Scania and South-East Sweden. Type A feet also occur in the White Sea District (table 11), but these designs are presumably unconnected with the innovation pattern of the type A foot designs of south-west Scandinavia. The difference in distribution suggests that the designs of naked and shod feet have separate innovation patterns, and different dates and significance.

That type A and B feet have a different symbolic significance is also suggested by the different ratios in which they tend to appear as pairs. Shoe designs occur much more commonly in pairs than do naked feet (table 12–13), especially in the northern regions. 63.5 % of type A feet were single, while 36.5 % occurred in pairs, but only 42 % of type B feet were single, with 58 % in pairs. In Ångermanland no less than 71.5 % of type B feet were in pairs.

A basis for dating type A foot designs is provided by the recent discovery of a stone slab from Vestre Løkke, Skjeberg, Østfold, which has an AIa1 foot design as well as the figure of a hand with four lines beyond the fingertips (fig. 20:2). This characteristic hand design is positively dated to Period 4 in Denmark by stone cists containing bronze objects (Chapter 9). Although there was no evidence of a burial at Vestre Løkke, the rectangular shape of the stone slab, and its dimensions (96×88×15 cm) show that it must have formed part of a burial cist.

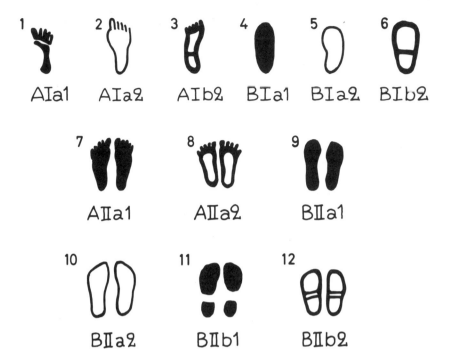

Fig. 21. Foot designs.
(Sites: 1: Järrestad nr 4, Scania. 2: Hjulatorp, Småland, South-East Sweden. 3: Tegneby, Bohuslän. 4: S. Härene, Västergötland, West Sweden. 5: Himmelstalund, Östergötland. 6: Åmøy, Rogaland. 7: Godensgård, Jylland, West Denmark. 8: Litsleby, Bohuslän. 9: Bahl, Jylland, West Denmark. 10: Lorensberg, Östergötland. 11: Godegården, Västergötland, West Sweden. 12: Järrestad nr 4, Scania.)

The conjunction of the hand motif and the type A foot design on the stone slab from Vestre Løkke reminds us of the fact that the two motifs have very similar distribution patterns (tables 10, 12 and 14). Both occur in the south-west; the hand motif from North Germany to Trøndelag and the type A foot from North Germany to Rogaland. It seems likely that they spread contemporaneously through the agency of the same innovation process.

A basis for dating the type B shoe design is provided by one of the stone slabs from Tuna, Ytterenhörna parish, Södermanland, in the Mälar District. It has two AIa1 ship designs and a pair of BIIb2 foot designs (provided that it is postulated that the right foot also originally had a cross strap) and should be dated to the Early Bronze Age (Montelius 1900, p. 190, fig. 1. Marstrander 1963, p. 226). Hammered-out BIIa1 foot designs occur on one of the slabs at the gable end of the cist found in a cairn at Myklabost, Sola parish, Rogaland (Fett 1941, pl. 38:B). This cist can probably also be assigned to the Early Bronze Age.

This chronological difference, with the positive dating of the naked type A foot to Period 4, and the probable dating of the first occurence of the shod type B foot to the Early Bronze Age, accords well with the chorological situation. If the two motifs, the naked foot and the shod foot, had been of the same age, it would follow that their distribution would also have been identical. This is not so. The hypothetical innovation pattern may thus be that the shoe design (type B) is the older motif, which spread in a fast, uninhibited innovation process up to Nämforsen (Ångermanland) and North Norway. The naked foot (type A) is a later motif which, together with the similarly hammered-out hand motif, appeared in Denmark in Period 4.

From Denmark it spread northwards along a westerly route. The innovation process was inhibited, perhaps because of a residual interest in the type B shoe design, and the type A foot occurs no further north than Rogaland-Hordaland.

The earliest form of the shoe design (type B) should be that which reached furthest north in the initial, swift innovation dissemination process. At Nämforsen, Ångermanland, and in North Norway, there are only contoured type B foot designs, most of which have cross straps (type Bb2). It has been established that type B foot designs occur much more often in pairs than do feet of type A, and further that as one moves northwards this tendency increases.

There are thus indications that the earliest foot designs were of type BIIb2, i.e. a pair of shoes, contoured and with a cross strap. This type is not found in Denmark. It does not occur further to the south-west than Scania, where the type probably originated. This presumably happened in Period 2–3, since the shoe designs must have had sufficient time to spread northwards before the process of innovation for the naked foot design began, in the transition between Periods 3 and 4.

It has already been suggested that the earliest clothing design, the kidney-shaped cloak, originated at the same time in the same area (i.e. Scania in Period 2–3) (chapter 8). It seemed likely that real sacrifices of cloaks in Denmark were replaced by engraved cloak images in Scania. Representations of feet of type B are normally of natural size. The sacrifice of shoes would in all probability consist of a pair of shoes, and we have already established on several occasions that shoe designs are far more likely to be found in pairs than are designs of the naked foot. We can therefore suggest that shoe designs, by analogy with representations of clothing, appeared in Period 2–3 in areas to the east of Denmark, as a reaction to Danish sacrificial customs.

In two of the log-coffin graves from the Early Bronze Age (the man's grave from Jels and the woman's grave from Skrydstrup), remains of leather footwear were found, in both cases secured by a strap round the instep (Broholm-Hald 1935, p. 291, and 1939, p. 85–86). Representations of feet of type B must therefore hypothetically depict the imprint of such footwear as made, for instance, in sand. These shoes—as they must properly be called—have in other log-coffin graves been replaced by pieces of cloth wrapped round the feet of the corpse. Shoes were, therefore, probably considered to be valuable. It is possible—and indeed probable—that both cloaks and shoes were among the many innovations made in the Early Bronze Age. Naturally they both appertained only to the rich. Their use as sacrifices—both in real life and in images—is thus quite natural.

It is more difficult to explain the emergence of the type A design, the naked foot. It appeared perhaps at the time of transition between Periods 3 and 4, based on the earlier type B, but influenced by the hand designs which were introduced at that time. The shoes were, so to speak, removed, and the naked foot invested with a new symbolic significance; either in conjunction with the symbolism of the hand designs, or perhaps only in a generally apotropaic sense.

10.3. Control corpus

10.3.1. North Germany

The material from North Germany consists of only five designs, of which three are of type A. There are no pairs (table 14–15). North Germany may therefore be considered along with the area in the south-west where type A foot designs are favoured, and where they rarely occur as pairs.

10.3.2. Scania

The control corpus, comprising 204 separate foot designs, is considerably larger than the original corpus of 151 designs. The ratio between type A and B designs, and between single feet and pairs, remains largely unaltered.

10.3.3. South-East Sweden

The number of foot designs has increased from 28 to 55, but as the number of ship designs has also increased from 66 to 211, the relative frequency of foot designs has decreased slightly to 26 %; this accords more closely with the values obtained in other areas in the east. Proportionately the relationship between types A and B and between I and II have remained fairly constant.

10.3.4. Östergötland

The control corpus consists of only 152 attributable foot designs, as against 180 in the original corpus. The qualitative determination remains largely unchanged. The addition of 6 % of type A foot designs in Öster-götland does not alter the thesis based on the original corpus that type A designs are primarily a feature of south-west Scandinavia.

10.3.5. Uppland

In the new literature there is an unmistakable type A foot design from Uppland (Kjellén-Hyenstrand 1976, fig. 36). The number of illustrated, attributable foot designs has risen from 14 to 70, which results in an increased relative frequency, from 10 % (in the Mälar District) to 44 % (in Uppland); this is contrary to the thesis proviously presented in this study, namely that the foot designs become less frequent towards the north-east. Kjellén and Hyenstrand have, however, published compre-hensive lists of the Uppland engravings, which are far more numerous than the illustrated material (1976, p. 116–117). According to these lists there are 305 foot designs and 1653 ship designs in Uppland, resulting in a ratio of 18.5 %. The new values now produce frequencies which con-tinually decrease from the south-west to the north-east: Scania 190.5 %, South-East Sweden 26 %, Östergötland 20.5 %, Uppland 18.5 % and Ångermanland 12.5 %.

10.3.6. Halland and Västergötland

A control corpus of 127 foot designs has been obtained for Halland and Västergötland, as against 158 designs in West Sweden in the original corpus. Nine type A foot designs, amounting to 7 %, fill the rather curious gap in the distribution of type A designs between Scania and Bohuslän.

10.3.7. Svenneby and Bottna

The 33 foot designs in Svenneby and Bottna in the control corpus are not among the 135 foot designs in the original corpus (cf. 4.5.6). However, the figures are comparable; thus, for instance, the foot designs have an unaltered low frequency: 6 % in Svenneby and Bottna, compared with 11.5 % in Bohuslän as a whole.

10.3.8. Hordaland

The control corpus consists of 62 foot designs from Hordaland, com-pared with only 6 in the original corpus from Middle Norway. This produces a foot design frequency as high as 58 % (as against 26.5 % from Trøndelag in the original corpus). Two type A feet are new; one of type AIa1 and the other of the rare type AIb2 (Mandt 1972, pl. 41: b and 40: a).

10.4. Foot designs at Nämforsen

Studies of ship designs at Nämforsen (table 6) established that the earliest ship designs occur at Notön (Nämforsen II) and Brådön (III). A similar topographical study of the foot designs demonstrates that this typically south Scandinavian motif is mainly concentrated in Brådön (table 16). It has already been remarked that the foot designs at Nämforsen (all shoe designs of type B) have a very marked tendency to occur in pairs; this is as high as 71.5 % (table 13). The relative frequency of foot designs is at the same time only 12.5 % (cf. 10.3.5). These circumstances must be interpreted to indicate that foot designs, in the form of type B shoes, early spread quickly northwards, and reached Nämforsen, probably as soon as the Early Bronze Age. Ship designs achieved longevity through the locally developed designs of type AIII. It is, however, evident that the engraving of shoe designs soon ceased. This difference in development would perhaps suggest that, whereas the late ship designs depicted types which occured locally, shoe designs had no corresponding local counterpart in real life.

11. Circles

11.1. Terminology and classification

These designs are by no means always geometrically accurate circles, but in the majority of cases this circumstance does not prevent correct classification. Some square figures with rounded corners have been found in Östergötland (Nordén 1925 A, p. 194, fig. 12–13); these are not catalogued as circles. On the site Järrestad 4, Scania, some type Bb shoe designs are depicted with two shoes in such close proximity that together they resemble a 'wheel-cross' (Althin 1945, Taf. 53). In this study figures which have concavities at one or both ends of a diameter are interpreted as Bb feet, while figures without such concavities are classified as circular designs.

The following typological elements can be distinguished. There may be no radii, four radii (i.e. two diameters), eight radii (i.e. four diameters) or some other number of radii. Sometimes the whole surface of the circle is hammered out; but as this kind of circle cannot be distinguished from a large cup-mark, or at least not in illustration (although a measurement of the depth of the engraving could perhaps provide a means of definition), they have had to be excluded from the present study, except where this feature is joined to a ship or a 'stand' (see below). In some cases the four radii of a circle are drawn with a double line. Lines which follow the direction of a radius, but do not extend to the centre of the circle are also counted as radii. Some circles enclose only radii, but in other cases one or more dots are also added. Alternatively the circle may contain other designs, sometimes with added dots. Simple circles must be seen in conjunction with those which are joined to a ship or stand. In order that a circle be seen as part of a ship the two motifs must be joined by at least one unbroken line (fig. 22:11).

The feature here described as a 'stand' can be defined as follows (fig. 22:13–15): a circle is said to have a stand if one, two or three lines join the periphery from the outside without cutting it. The maximum distance between the outermost lines which make up the stand, at the point of contact with the circle, must not exceed a third of the circumference of the circle. The length of the stand measured radially from the circle must not exceed four times the circle's diameter. At the bottom, i.e. furthest away from the circle, the stand can either be open, or closed by a crosswise line: further crosswise or oblique lines may be present.

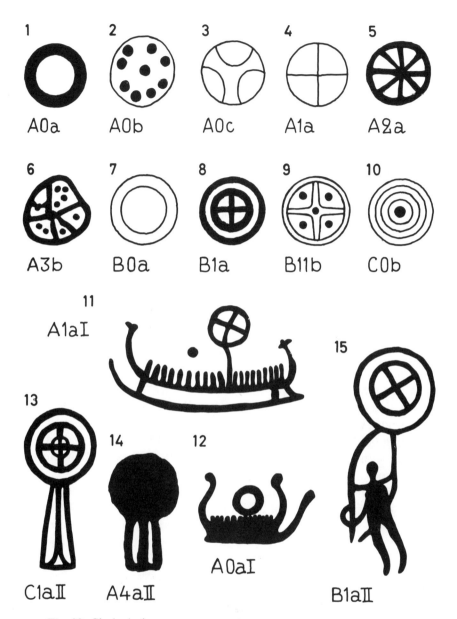

Fig. 22. Circle designs.
(Sites: *1:* Engelstrup, Sjælland, West Denmark. *2:* Skjeberg, Østfold. *3:* Hjulatorp, Småland, South-East Sweden. *4:* Kivik, Scania. *5:* Herrebro, Östergötland. *6:* Nibehøj, Jylland, West Denmark. *7:* Nag, Rogaland. *8:* Lille Strandegård, Bornholm. *9:* Fossum, Telemark, Middle Norway. *10:* Herrebro, Östergötland. *11:* Bottna, Bohuslän. *12:* Tegneby, Bohuslän. *13:* Backa in Brastad, Bohuslän. *14:* Karetski Noss, Onega District. *15:* Backa in Brastad, Bohuslän.)

These features may be considered with the aid of a system of fourteen typological elements, expressed by means of the following symbols.

A   A circle.
B   Two concentric circles.
C   Three or more concentric circles.
0   No radii
1   Four radii (= two diameters) drawn with single lines.
11 Four radii (= two diameters) drawn with double lines.
2   Eight radii (= four diameters).
3   A number of radii other than zero, four or eight.
4   A hammered-out circle.
a   No designs except radii within the circle.
b   One or more dots within the circle (possibly including radii).
c   Designs other than dots and radii within the circle (but possible including either or both).
I   Circle joined to a ship.
II Circle with a stand.

11.2. Chorology and chronology

Table 17–19 list the circular designs of the original corpus. The numbers are large: there are 648 circles, of which 575 are separate, 24 joined to ships and 49 to stands. The figures show that 30 examples of the latter form come from the Onega District. Table 17 shows the geographical distribution of the circular designs. Unusually, West Denmark leads with 119 designs, followed by Bohuslän with 100, Östergötland with 71, Rogaland with 60, Scania with 52 and Østfold with 47 designs. These areas, together with West Denmark and Scania, are the richest areas in Northern Europe.

These relationships become even clearer when the circular designs are expressed as a percentage of the ship designs (table 17). West Denmark has the highest total, 457.5 % (i.e. circular designs are four and a half times as common as ship designs), followed by South Finland and the Onega District with 115 %, Middle Norway 66 %, West Sweden 55.5 %, Scania 46.5 % and Bornholm 41.5 %. Disregarding the Onega District, which in this as in so many other instances holds a unique position, it is evident that circular designs are definitely a feature of the south and west. It is most remarkable that it is the *poor* areas in the west—West Sweden and Middle Norway—which are relatively rich in circular designs, while the rich areas—Bohuslän, Østfold, Rogaland and Trøndelag—have low relative percentages: 8.5 %, 15 %, 12 % and 13 % respectively. Even the rich area in the east, Östergötland, has the low percentage of 11 %, followed, as in so many other instances, by the Mälar District with 7.5 %.

The eleven elements which define the types of unconnected circular designs—excluding therefore I (circle joined to a ship), II (circle with a stand) and 4 (hammered-out circle, which is only admitted in combination with I and II)—have a capacity of 45 theoretically possible types. Twenty-seven are actually represented in our material: 13 type A (plain circles), 8 type B (two concentric circles), and 6 type C (three or more concentric circles). Of possible type A designs only two are absent: types A11c and A3c. Table 17, however, shows only the nine most common types, which are represented by more than 10 examples each.

Such a rich variety of types might suggest a fairly equal division of circular design types, as is the case with ship designs, where the most common type, AIa1, only accounts for 14 % of all ship designs. But the opposite is in fact true: the commonest type of circular design. A1a (a circle with four radii and no additional features) is represented by no less than 251 examples or 38.5 % of the whole material. The next, type A0a, occurs in 112 examples or 17.5 % of the whole. Much less common is A0b with 38 examples, C0a with 31 examples and B0a with 26 examples. All these five common types are simple in comparison with some other types of far more complicated design. The five common types account for 70.5 % of the corpus, and the earliest type of circular design is probably to be found among them. If this is indeed so, then the innovation process must have differed from that which applied to the ship and foot designs.

Tables 18–19 illustrate the chorology of the elements which define the types. It can be seen that element A (a plain circle) predominates in West Denmark with 94 %, Scania 90.5 %, Bornholm 94.5 % and West Sweden 96 %; the values of the latter areas being naturally less reliable owing to the relatively small number of examples. The single circle is therefore primarily a South Scandinavian phenomenon. It is interesting that Ångermanland has 100 % type A designs, even if this figure is based on only two examples. As is so often the case, South Finland and the Onega District are conspicuous exceptions to the norm.

In South-East Sweden, Östergötland, the Mälar District, Bohuslän, Østfold, South Norway, Rogaland, Middle Norway and Trøndelag elements B (two concentric circles) and C (three and more concentric circles) account for more than 15 % and up to 58.5 %, but in Denmark only for 3 %. Two and more concentric circles is thus chiefly a northern phenomenon.

The radii elements 0 (no radii) and 1 (four radii) predominate with 87.5 %. Elements 2 (eight radii) and 3 (a number of radii other than zero, four or eight) are fairly evenly distributed throughout all the areas in small numbers. Element 11 (a simple double-line cross) is exclusive to South Norway. Element 4 (a hammered-out circle, joined to a ship or with a stand) predominates in the Onega District, but also occurs in Bohuslän. The most significant feature is the chorological contrast between elements 0 and 1, which are fairly equally represented. Disregarding the poor areas of North Norway and Ångermanland and the exceptional Onega District, element 1 (four radii) is in the majority in Denmark, Scania, Östergötland, and Bohuslän. Element 0 (no radii) predominates in Norway. The simple cross is therefore a feature of the south and to some extent of the east, while the circle without radii is a feature of the northwest.

Additions in the form of dots and figures within the circle (elements b and c) are infrequent in Denmark (11 %), Scania (0 %) and West Sweden (15.5 %). Percentages of 30 %, 21 % and 39.5 % for Rogaland, Middle Norway and Trøndelag respectively are remarkable because of the relative wealth of these areas. It is clear, therfore, that these elements are primarily a feature of the north and in particular of the north-west.

Circles which are joined to ships or stands (elements I and II) are in the first place associated with Bohuslän which has 26 %, followed by Östfold 6.5 %, Rogaland 8 %, Östergötland 6 %, and to a smaller extent with Trøndelag, 5 %. The complex structures involving circles are thus characteristic of the northern innovation centres.

To recapitulate: circles and radii are distributed throughout Northern Europe, whereas other additions and complex structures are primarily northern phenomena. Element A (a single circle) predominates most strongly in Denmark and Scania, together with elements 1 (four radii) and a (no additions). In West Denmark type A1a accounts for 65.5 % of all circular designs, and in Scania the figure is 67.5 %.

Is it possible that the circular designs originated in West Denmark, where their frequency is relatively the largest (457.5 % of the number of ships)? Type A1a (a circle with four radii), which holds a unique position of strength in West Denmark, is a plausible prototype, from which it is easy to imagine the development both of the single circle without radii (type A0a), circles with many radii and other additions, and multi-concentric circles. But, if this is so, the innovation process of circular designs must have been different from that of foot designs and, in particular, from that of the ships. In West Denmark ship designs, particularly the earliest type, AIa1, are relatively rare. Circular designs are on the contrary common, especially the earliest type A1a. The most plausible hypothesis is one which postulates that many examples of type A1a (a circle with four radii) were engraved in West Denmark because it is an early design which continued to be appreciated for a long time, its symbolic meaning being so obvious that there was resistance to change. At the same time the circular motif had little influence in other areas; its innovation processes were perhaps inhibited by the fact that the symbolism seemed obscure in the northern areas. If the symbolic meaning of the circular motif largely eludes our understanding, we can at least theorise concerning its origins. The wheels depicted on representations of carts correspond completely to the definitions of the circular design types. The carts with four-spoked wheels are the earliest (fig. 16:1) and they agree with the definition of circle type A1a. All 16 cart designs in Skåne have these four-spoked wheels (table 7 together with 5.2). In Bohuslän and Østfold, however, the most common cart wheel designs are the plain circle, the circle with a dot in the centre, and the two concentric circles; these correspond to circle designs type A0a, A0b and B0a. On the other hand no cart designs have wheels shown as circles with eight, or an odd number, of radii, or with the addition of dots or other figures (fig. 22: 2–3, 5–6); that is, those figures which occur particularly in the northern areas. One must therefore conclude that the circle motif was originally a simple portrayal of a four-spoked wheel. The Trundholm cart (Broholm 1952 A, fig. 199) proves that four-spoked wheels did in fact exist in Early Bronze Age Denmark. There has never been any doubt that the gilt disc carried on this cart represents the sun. But this sun symbol is *not* decorated with a cross. Consequently it is clear that in Period 2 in Denmark, a circular design of type A1a (fig. 22:4), the most common and probably the earliest type of such designs, is associated with the cart wheel, whereas it cannot be demonstrated that it symbolises the sun. The fact that less interest is shown in circular designs in the northern areas and that there is here a tendency to make the designs less wheel-like by various changes and additions, could be explained if carts and wheels were more unusual in the north than in the south.

The differences between the innovation processes of ship and circle designs can, therefore, be interpreted to mean that the ship motif spread with an uninhibited diffusion process because the symbolism was understood everywhere (and sometimes led to ship designs being changed into more realistic representations of local ship types). The diffusion process of the circular motif on the other hand became inhibited because an insufficient understanding of carts and wheels in northern areas prevented this motif from becoming popular.

The Wismar trumpet provides a basis for dating the circular designs, since the trumpet has eight of them in pairs in the fourth panel from the bell (fig. 5:4). All consists of two concentric circles and have four radii. Four of them have a dot or a (slightly angular) small ring in the centre. They may therefore be identified as of type B1b. The four circles which have no central dot are of type B1a. Type B (two concentric circles) was therefore known in Period 3. On the seventh ornamental panel of the trumpet there are concentric circles which are formally of type C0a.

The Kivik cist provides further dating evidence in that type A1a circles occur on slabs four and six (fig. 6). The wheels of the cart on slab seven are of the same design (fig. 16:1). The presumed prototype (A1a) is therefore found as early as Period 3.

Good dating evidence is provided by a stone cist in a barrow from Glatved, Hoed parish, Jutland, which contained a brooch and knife of

Period 3. One of the roof slabs displays at least three circles of type A1a. (Glob 1969, p. 240. Ramskou 1952, p. 132). On a slab at the gable end of a stone cist in one of the large barrows at Rege, Sola parish, Jæren in Rogaland there is a circular design of type C0a (Fett 1941, pl. 38: C). The rich grave goods are usually dated to the end of Period 2. But the barrow was excavated as early as 1882, and an adjacent cist contained what may be a secondary burial from the Late Bronze Age (Marstrander 1963, p. 270. Hagen 1967, p. 114. Lund 1934, p. 49). It is possible, therefore, that the cist with the decorated slab was also uncovered later than Period 2.

The evidence leaves no room for doubt that the circular designs can be referred to the Early Bronze Age, perhaps to Period 2. It is clear that type A1a, the single circle with four radii, is early in the series, and there is nothing in the finds to contradict the assumption that this was the prototype. The Balkåkra 'drum' and the wheel-headed pins which were also imported (these often correspond to the definition of circular designs type B2a) demonstrate that a source of inspiration for circular designs associated with magic and ritual existed in South Scandinavia as early as Period 1 (Montelius 1917, fig. 847. Broholm 1952 B, fig. 41). The fact that circular designs of type B2a are very rare in rock art, and do not occur at all in Denmark and Scania, may be seen as indicative of the fact that the actual prototype was less complicated. The wheels on the Trundholm cart from Period 2, for instance, accord very well with type A1a.

11.3. Control corpus

11.3.1. North Germany

Tables 20–21 list the 336 circular designs of the control corpus. The North German material consists of only nine designs; a statistical analysis of the relationship between the elements is therefore of doubtful value. It is clear, however, that North Germany differs from the southern Scandinavian areas (Denmark, Scania and other areas in the south), for in these areas element A (a circle) and 1 (four radii) predominate. Although element A is commoner in North Germany than element B, it is proportionately less common than in Denmark and Scania, whilst element 0 (no radii) is commoner than 1, which is otherwise typical of northern areas. Element b (dots in the circle) is likewise strongly represented both in the northern areas and in North Germany. These features, which differ from those recorded in Denmark and Scania, may perhaps suggest that North Germany was not part of the area of origin of the circular designs.

11.3.2. Scania

The 67 designs of the control corpus produce a pattern which is similar to that of the 52 designs in the original corpus.

11.3.3. South-East Sweden

The control corpus consists of only 14 designs as against 21 in the original corpus. The ratio between the elements is approximately the same as in the original corpus. However, in the control corpus element 0 (no radii) is more common than 1 (four radii); thus South-East Sweden stands out as a more peripheral area.

11.3.4. Östergötland

Both the control and original corpuses consist of 71 circular designs. The elements which characterise the central areas (A, 1 and a) have become slightly less frequent, but the correlation is otherwise good.

11.3.5. Uppland

The control corpus consists of 23 designs from Uppland, as against 10 from the Mälar District in the original corpus. As is often the case, the relative positions of the elements closely follow the pattern found in Östergötland. With only 52 % of element A, Uppland emerges, together with Hordaland, as the most peripheral area in the control corpus.

Kjellén-Hyenstrand's statistics list 135 circular designs in Uppland (Kjellén-Hyenstrand 1976, p. 117). As 1653 ship designs are listed in the same source, the relative frequency of the circular designs is 8 %. This confirms the scarcity of this motif in the north-easterly areas.

11.3.6. Halland and Västergötland

The control corpus comprises 34 circular designs, as against 26 from the whole of West Sweden in the original corpus. Halland–Västergötland retains the character of an area, which is closely associated with Denmark, and with an increased share of elements A, 1 and a.

11.3.7. Svenneby and Bottna

There are 44 circular designs from Svenneby and Bottna, none of which occur in the original corpus, which consisted of 100 designs from the whole of Bohuslän. The relative frequency (in relation to ship designs) is 8 % for the control corpus and 8.5 % for the original corpus. Thus Bohuslän still appears to be poor in circular designs. In Svenneby and Bottna, as in Bohuslän generally, circular designs are very often found joined to ships or stands. The control corpus confirms that Bohuslän has a large share in elements A and a, while element 0 (no radii) is strongly featured and even predominates over element 1 (four radii).

11.3.8. Hordaland

Seventy-four circular designs from Hordaland are recorded in the control corpus, while the original corpus consisted of 33 designs from the whole of Middle Norway. The relative frequency (in relation to ships) is maintained: 69 % in the control corpus as compared to 66 % in the original corpus. Clearly, then, the poor area of Middle Norway (including Hordaland) has a high ratio of circular designs, while the rich Rogaland area has a low ratio—this corresponds to the high ratios recorded in the poor area of West Sweden (including Halland–Västergötland) and the low ratios in the rich area of Bohuslän (including Svenneby and Bottna). Hordaland, with low frequencies of elements A, 1 and a, is seen as a typical peripheral area. With regard to the frequency of elements, this area correlates almost equally well with the Rogaland and Middle Norway areas of the original corpus.

11.4. Circular designs at Nämforsen

There are only two circular designs at Nämforsen, both of type A1a (Hallström 1960, Pl. 12 and 25) one is from the river banks (Nämforsen I) and the other from Brådön (Nämforsen III). Circular designs are therefore at least present on the central Brådön, where the earliest ship designs (4.7) and most of the foot designs (10.4) also occur.

It has already been established that the circular designs must have spread northwards from Denmark through an inhibited innovation process. But this interpretation cannot be applied to the engravings at Nämforsen, since it is clear that early ship, foot and circular designs reached this site quickly. This suggests that the nature of the innovation process was not one of a gradual northward movement through the Scandinavian peninsula. On the contrary, there seems to have been direct contact between South Scandinavia and Nämforsen. Such rapid direct contact would not only explain the early character of the designs, but also their subsequent development. The interest in foot and circular designs was soon lost at Nämforsen, but representations of ships seem to have been redesigned to make them more realistic images of local boat types, which attained lasting popularity.

11.5. The principal trends of the chorology

It has been established in the preceeding chapters that a zone to the east of West Denmark—in particular Scania, West Sweden, Bohuslän and Østfold—is characterised by a preponderance of engraved scenes, evidently portraying ritual ceremonies of various kinds. It is possible that the ceremonies depticted in this way were actually performed in Denmark.

An east Swedish zone lies further from Denmark: although extending as far as Scania, it is centred on Östergötland and the Mälar District. This zone is characterised by a particular interest in weapon and clothing designs drawn to a natural scale. It is likely that these images portray objects which were actually sacrificed in Denmark and in the western zone.

Circular designs also permit an analysis of the rock engravings in Denmark. The main interest here is in more abstract symbols, like the four-spoked wheel. The naked foot and the hand (with four lines in front of the fingertips) also belong in this category. Ship designs with added crew lines also in a sense belong in this group. The crew lines were apparently not explicit enough in Bohuslän, where realistic human figures were added as crew or acrobats in a rather incongruous manner. In these cases it is doubtful whether the artist fully appreciated that the crew lines represented human beings. The circular designs of Denmark differ from those of Bohuslän/Østfold, in that the latter are made more tangible by mounting the circles on stands or ships.

The cup-mark is an even more abstract figure than the circle. Cup-marks fall outside the framework of the present study, primarily because they are unevenly and often inadequately published. In the original 1972 version of this study, the author found that as a result of his work on the original corpus he could postulate that cup-marks are relatively very common in Denmark; recent literature supports this thesis. In Denmark 14 % of rock-engraving sites have figure designs, while 86 % have cup-marks only. In Scania 10 % of the sites have figure designs, while 90 % have cupmarks only. In Uppland 27 % of the sites have figure designs and 73 % cup-marks only, and in Hordaland two thirds of the sites, or about 66 % have cup-marks only. (Mandt 1972, p. 72). The high frequency of cup-marks in South Scandinavia is further demonstrated by the fact that cup-marks also occur on 20 of the 27 sites in Scania which had figure designs, i.e. on three-quarters of these sites (Welinder 1974, p. 253).

There is, therefore, evidence to suggest that the cup-marks conform to the general distribution of abstract motifs in rock art, in that they are more common in southern areas and particularly in Denmark, than in the north.

12. The human figure

12.1. Terminology and classification

The human figure in rock art is rich in typological elements and also more evocative than most other motifs. The classification is based on such elements as can be registered objectively and easily and are present in most or all of the figures.

Most human figures have two clearly-drawn *legs*. Figures where the calf is clearly marked (fig. 23:8 and 10–11) may be distinguished from those where the legs are of uniform thickness (fig. 23:4). An *accentuated calf* is one where the calf is at least one and a half times as wide as the narrowest part of the leg.

Both *arms* (fig. 23:1) or only one arm may be visible, or there may be no arms (fig. 23:10). In the latter case it may be that the man is portrayed as wrapped in a cloak (Almgren 1960, p. 30). There may be *fingers* (fig. 23: 3 and 5) or just a thumb protruding from the hand (Althin 1945, Taf. 57), as with the separate hand signs (chapter 9 above). For the purpose of this study, figures with arms which divide at the ends are defined as having fingers.

A division between male and female figures might seem appropriate, as the sex organs are often clearly marked. Phallic figures are easily distinguished as males, as are presumably those figures with clearly-drawn weapons. All other figures are to some extent ambiguous. The sex organ of the woman in the copulation scene on a round stone disc from Maltegård, Sjælland, West Denmark (fig. 23:3. Glob 1969, fig. 102:a) is marked by a short vertical line, but the same convention (fig. 23:1) is sometimes interpreted in the literature as indicating a male (Marstrander 1963, p. 201). The head of the woman on the Maltegård disc is drawn in the same way as that of the man, but in similar scenes from Bohuslän it seems that the woman is represented with long hair (Baltzer 1881–90, pl. 19). On the other hand, some sword-bearing, phallic figures from Østfold have heads drawn in a similar manner, apparently with long hair at the back of the neck (fig. 23:11). For these reasons no distinction is made in the present study between male and female figures, but only between *phallic* and *non-phallic* figures.

Most of the Scandinavian human figures are represented *standing*, and there are no difficulties in identifying other positions, such as sitting or acrobatic postures (fig. 23:9); all these are included under the heading of *not standing*.

Fig. 23. Human figures.
(Sites: *1:* Store Dal, Østfold. *2:* Aspeberget, Bohuslän. *3:* Maltegård.
Sjælland, West Danmark. *4:* Herrestrup, Sjælland, West-Danmark. *5:*
Vitlycke, Bohuslän. *6:* Kivik, Scania. *7:* Leonardsberg, Östergötland.
8: Vitlycke, Bohuslän. *9:* Tanum, Bohuslän. *10:* Backa in Brastad,
Bohuslän. *11:* Navestad, Østfold. *12:* Kivik, Scania. *13:* Tegneby,
Bohuslän.)

About half the human figures are accompanied by an *attribute*, which is carried and usually identifiable as a weapon. These must be attached to the figure by the unbroken lines of the drawing.

A *sword* is identified here as a single line running obliquely downwards from the back of the figure. It must not extend beneath a horizontal line taken from the lowest part of the legs (or feet) (fig. 23:2, 4–8 and 11). The hilt of the sword sometimes extends to the front of the body; for instance, the cross-shaped hilt on fig. 24:8. For the interpretation of these figures it is no doubt important to note that men are never represented with drawn swords in their hands.

It would be possible to define the concept of an *axe* in writing, but it would be a long definition. This is not, however, necessary as the designs clearly and unequivocally show that what is portrayed is an axe and nothing else. The following comments on fig. 23:5 and 8 will therefore suffice. The handle of the axe can be a simple extension of the arm, or it can be at an angle to the arm; where the handle and the arm join, fingers may be indicated. The head of the axe is clearly marked, the edge always facing forwards.

A *spear* is defined as a line, with or without a lancet-shaped or triangular forward-pointing head, at oblique or right angels (but not parallel) to the vertical axis of the body. The spear is either held in the hand (fig. 23:13) or (in armless figures) consists of a line at an angle to the body (Baltzer 1881–90, pl. 56:6).

For reasons explained above with regard to axes, the *bow* can best be defined by reference to fig. 23:2; it is a narrow, frame-like vertical design divided in the centre by a horizontal line.

A *shield* may be round or rectangular. A round shield is defined as a circular design immediately above the legs of the human figure. It may be either a plain circle (fig. 23:2), several concentric circles (fig. 23:5), a circle crossed by two diameters or a hammered-out circle. A rectangular shield is always hammered-out and held in the hand (fig. 23:13).

A human figure on the back of a quadruped is called a *rider* provided that the man and the animal are joined by a continuous line. The rider may have no legs (fig. 23:13) or he may be portrayed with legs, standing on the back of the animal (Althin 1945, Taf. 60); occasionally the rider's legs extend below the body of the animal (Baltzer 1881–90, Pl. 44:3).

It has not been possible to isolate any other attribute within the framework of the present study. All other objects associated with human figures by unbroken lines are collected under the heading of *other attributes*. Rectangular shields have been included under this heading for the purpose of chorological studies. A variety of such attributes may be observed in Baltzer's illustrations of rock art from Bohuslän: human figures apparently carrying a ship (Baltzer 1881–90, Pl. 45:1); carrying a circular design on a stand (Pl. 9:1 cf. fig. 22:15 in this study); carrying a vertical staff (Pl. 49:8); blowing trumpets (Pl 58:3); and human figures apparently sitting on a swing (Pl. 40:5).

The typological elements defined above can be expressed by means of the following eighteen symbols:

A   Legs with no calves and at least one arm.
B   Legs with no calves and no arms.
C   Legs with accentuated calves and at least one arm.
D   Legs with accentuated calves and no arms.
E   Without legs but with other human features.
I   Standing, non-phallic.
II   Standing, phallic.
III   Not standing, non-phallic.
a   Without fingers.
b   With fingers.
0   Without attributes.
1   With sword.
2   With axe.
3   With spear.
4   With bow.
5   With shield.
6   With other attributes.
7   Rider.

In spite of the deliberate limitation of the number of symbols the capacity of the classification system is considerable. Elements B and D (without arms) cannot be combined with a and b (fingers). If we assume that a human figure can have only one of the attributes 0–7 (which is not the case) we arrive at ta total of $48+24+48+24=144$ theoretically possible types. If two attributes are assigned to each figure the number of possible types becomes as great as 522. The human figure is more variable than any other design in rock art.

12.2. Chorology and chronology

The material compiled by the author from the source literature amounts to 1034 human figures. It does not include five carts with drivers (table 7, types A1a and A3c), five scenes of ploughing with ploughmen (chapter 6), or 43 figures carrying weapons: in these cases the weapons were judged to have been depicted at approximately natural size, while the men are in miniature (table 8, types A3, S3 and E3). Among the 1034 designs, figures with weapons are included where the men and the weapons are to the *same* scale, whether to approximate natural size or in miniature.

Table 22 shows that among the geographical areas Bohuslän leads with 422 human figures; Östergötland has 100 and Trøndelag 75. West Denmark is among the poorer areas with only ten figures, while Scania is rich with 42 such designs.

As usual, the ratio of human figures to ship designs provides a clearer picture (last column, table 22). The unusually high percentage of 47 % in the Mälar district is due to particular shortcomings in the original corpus for this area. Kjellén's and Hyenstrand's figures for Uppland (1976, p. 117) give 187 human figure designs and 1653 ship designs, a proportion of only 11.5 %. The south-western areas have a high frequency of human figures: West Denmark 38.5 %, Scania 37.5 % and Bohuslän 36.5 %. Low frequencies occur in the eastern areas: South-East Sweden 0 %, Bornholm 2 %, Östergötland 15.5 % and Uppland (according to Kjellén's statistics) 11.5 %.

Remarkably low frequencies are recorded from Østfold (16 %), South Norway (14 %) and Rogaland (1.5 %). North of Rogaland, however, the frequencies increase again: Middle Norway has 20 %, Trøndelag 26 % and North Norway 66.5 %. Mandt's new figures for Hordaland (1972, p. 73) accord well with this group: 75 human designs, 163 ship designs, or 46 %. In the north-east the percentages are also high: Ångermanland 24 % and Finland-Karelia 104.5 %.

This distribution, with a marked preference for human figure designs in south-westerly and north-easterly regions, and with less interest in the wide intermediate zone, invites the conclusion that the human figure designs do not represent a uniform system, but are the result of two different traditions.

Table 22 shows the eleven most common types, which are represented by more than 20 examples each. Together they represent 72.5 % of the whole material. Only the *number* of attributes (elements 0 and 1–7) is shown in the table thus: 0, + or ++. The specific atributes are not indicated as this would have unreasonably increased the size of the table. Types with three attributes (shown in tables 23 and 24 as +++) are rare, and occur mainly in Bohuslän.

Most common by far is type AIa0 (a figure with arms and legs without calves, standing, non-phallic, without fingers or attributes). It is represented by 288 examples (28 % of the whole material) and is fairly evenly distributed over the whole North European area. Other common types are BIa0 (figures without arms, but otherwise as AIa0) and BIa+ (like BIa0 but with one attribute). These types have, however, a different distribution pattern to AIa0: they do not occur in Denmark or the north-eastern areas, but are concentrated to Scania, Östergötland, the Mälar District and Bohuslän.

The chorological variations of the human figure designs can best be seen in table 24, which shows the distribution in percentages of the elements defining the types.

Accentuated calves (elements C and D) occur mainly in Bohuslän (31.5 %) and Østfold (31 %), but are absent in Denmark and rare in Scania and Östergötland.

The 'poor' type B designs (without arms and legs without calves) are concentrated to the eastern areas: Scania (33.5 %) and Östergötland (36 %). In Uppland (the Mälar District), according to Kjellén and Hyenstrand (1977, p. 71), the human figures usually also lack arms, but have strongly accentuated calves and therefore belong to type D. Considering the hypothesis that armless figures are representations of a man wrapped in a cloak, it is noteworthy that the full-size representations of cloaks mainly occur in these eastern areas—Scania, Östergötland and Uppland (cf. chapter 8).

Type E (without legs) is most common in Scania and Bohuslän, which areas together account for 82 % of the total number (cf. table 23). The type comprises a rather mixed group of designs, including riders (fig. 23: 13) and the figures in the Kivik grave which, according to a plausible hypothesis, are dressed in garments reaching down to the ground (fig. 23: 12). The absence of legs does not imply immobility: indeed, these figures are a typical example of the tendency to make dramatic designs which characterises the areas to the east of West Denmark.

Element II (phallic figures) has a westerly distribution in Scandinavia, where it is mainly characteristic of West Denmark (30 %), Bohuslän (43 %), Østfold (15.5 %) and Trøndelag (25.5 %). In the east the phallic element is weaker: Scania 2.5 % (14.5 % if the phallic axebearing men are included), Östergötland 6 % and the Mälar District 0 %. The new publications from Uppland (Kjellén and Hyenstrand 1977 p. 71) confirm that the phallic element is rare in this area, although it does occasionally occur. In the White Sea District the phallic element reappears in no less than 43 % of the figures, once again arousing doubts about the connection with South Scandinavia. It seems evident, however, that there is a positive correlation between the phallic element and interest in the human figure designs in general.

Element III (not standing) usually relates to acrobats and other figures in violent motion (fig. 23:9); it belongs almost exclusively to Bohuslän (table 23), and once more demonstrates the penchant for the dramatic in areas along the eastern Kattegatt coast.

Delineated fingers (element b, fig. 23:3 and 5) are mainly found in some western areas: West Denmark (40 %), Bohuslän (9 %), Østfold (8 %) and Trøndelag (8 %). Fingers are depicted on the only petroglyph with human figures in North Germany, the stone cist from Anderlingen (Capelle 1972, p. 235, Abb. 11). This distribution correlates with that of hand designs (table 10), which also occur in the same areas as well as in Rogaland and Middle Norway. The delineated fingers may therefore have a significance beyond demonstrating that the axe is held in the hand.

55 % of the human figures have no attributes (element 0). Most areas, however, have a higher proportion of figures without attributes. A few areas have a low proportion: Scania (55 %) Bohuslän (41 %) and the

White Sea District (25 %). As attributes undoubtedly create an increased sense of action, the greater interest shown in the dramatic treatment of rock art in West Denmark's eastern neighbours—Scania and Bohuslän—is further confirmed. Bohuslän is unique in that 20.5 % of its figures possess two or three attributes. The abundance of attributes in Finland-Karelia must have a different origin.

The sword (element 1) is the most common attribute. The highest frequency is that of Bohuslän (40 %), followed by Östergötland (34 %), which is also the only area with full-size sword designs which are not carried (table 8).

Axes (element 2) are found only in Bohuslän (9 %), Østfold and North Germany. It must be remembered, however, that full-size axes, carried by men in miniature (table 8, type A 3), also occur in Scania (the only area with this type of design). The difference in intention need not be great: in Bohuslän it is the gesture that is emphasised, in Scania it is the axe itself.

In Scandinavia, spears (element 3) occur as attributes mainly in Bohuslän and Östergötland (table 23). These are the areas which also account for most of the full-size spears which are either not carried or carried by men in miniature (table 8). In Denmark the spear is recorded only once, in a lively hunting scene on a stone barely 10 cm long found at Bjergager-gård, Jutland (Glob 1969, p. 100, fig. 105); this is the part of Denmark closest to Bohuslän. It is one of the few cases where a rock-engraving may have been imported.

Apart from the White Sea District, the bow (element 4) occurs only rarely in Bohuslän and Østfold and in the Sagaholm cist (fig. 15:42), which was recently found in South-East Sweden very close to the Öster-götland border (and not included in tables 22–24).

The shield (element 5) occurs in Östergötland, the Mälar District, Bohuslän, Østfold and South Norway, a fairly well-grouped area. The high percentage recorded for the Mälar District in the original corpus is confirmed by Kjellén and Hyenstrand (1977, p. 71), who give the number of shield-bearers as at least 30. There is no reason to question the interpretation of these figures as shield-bearers, even though the shields are much larger (Kjellén and Hyenstrand 1977, p. 74, fig. 66–67) than those in Bohuslän (fig. 23:5). Hypotheses involving a multifolded sun god or a magic sun calendar appear to have no factual basis.

Riders (element 7) occur in Scania, Bohuslän and Trøndelag, a fairly typical distribution for so dramatic a motif. A few isolated rider designs also occur in Østfold (Marstrander 1963, p. 231, fig. 58:6). Most of the rider designs seem to represent acrobats, with or without reins, standing on the backs of the horses (Althin 1945, Taf. 60). The rider designs in Bohuslän, on the other hand, are of type E1a367 (or close variants): a human figure without legs or fingers, on horseback, with a spear and another attribute, which is usually interpreted as a rectangular shield, lifted above the head (fig. 23:13). The rock-engraving at Tegneby Mellangården (Baltzer 1881–90, Pl. 30:3) is usually confidently interpreted as a deliberately designed battle scene, unique among the rock art of Bohuslän. This interpretation is of course possible, but not self-evident. Several groups of ship designs could by the same token be interpreted as depicting sea-battles, and were indeed so interpreted in the infancy of rock art research. One feature of this unusual rock-engraving, which is of importance for dating, and perhaps also for interpretation, is the standing human figure on the far right: it has accentuated calves and carries the same weapons as the riders—a spear and what is thought to be a rectangular shield. The figure is of type CIa36. There is no doubt, therefore, that the riders belong to a period when human figures with accentuated calves were also produced in Bohuslän. Almost one third of all figures in this area possess this attribute.

Element 6 (other attributes) is recorded in appreciable numbers in Scania, Östergötland and, above all, in Bohuslän and Finland-Karelia. It is obvious that 'other attributes' occur most frequently in areas where the human figure is represented in many variations, but also in such areas where the designs differ greatly from the norm which formed the basis for the selection of elements 1–5 and 7.

There is some basis for dating human figures. The Wismar trumpet (fig. 5) and stones 7 and 8 of the Kivik cist (fig. 6) provide a natural starting-point. Here, as early as Period 3, we find types AIa0, AIa6, BIa0, BIa1, BIa35, BIa6 and EIa0. These are human figures with and without arms, with and without legs and with sword, spear, shield and trumpet. Designs *not* exemplified here are accentuated calves (elements C and D), fingers (b), phallic figures (II) and figures not standing (III).

Thus accentuated calves apparently did not occur in the earliest phase of Scandinavian rock art, but it was presumably not long before this feature was introduced. It can be observed that the human figures on the Kivik stones have slightly curved lower legs, a design which may be the precursor of the later accentuated calves. The bronze sculptures in the well-known hoard from Stockhult, Scania, display a similar rendering of calves as early as period 2 (Montelius 1917, fig. 981). The same manner of drawing legs is seen on the end stone in the cist from Anderlingen, North Germany (Capelle 1972, p. 235, Abb. 11), which probably dates from the early Bronze Age. This leg design is again seen in the Sagaholm grave (fig. 15:30 and 42), dated by the grave type as well as by C14 to the Early Bronze Age (4.6.3).

The Sagaholm figures are phallic, unlike those at Kivik and Anderlingen. Is it then possible that the phallic element characterised the human figure from the beginning? Perhaps not. It is of course impossible to determine the exact relationship between the dates of Kivik and Sagaholm. The chronological relationship between Bronze Age monuments and artefacts in Scania and their eqvivalents in Östergötland is generally not accurately established. Along with other late features all ship designs in Sagaholm are, however, of type C, which is secondary to type A designs represented in Kivik; it is therefore most likely that Sagaholm is later than Kivik.

The dating of the phallic element can also be discussed on the basis of such axe-bearers as those on the rock-engraving Simris no. 19 in Scania (fig. 18:2). The axe carried by these figures is often classified as a flanged axe, which indicates a date as far back as period 1. In such a case the human figure designs must have appeared at the same time as the ship designs on the Rørby sword. Against this identification it can be argued that a similar axe is depticted on the Kivik stone no. 1 (fig. 6). The axe type can therefore not provide a date for Simris no 19 which is earlier than that for Kivik.

The rock-engravings from Truehøjgård, Jutland (Glob 1969, fig. 18:d) may be used as some kind of reference for the dating of the phallic element: it has been assigned to period 3 but may perhaps belong to period 4 (cf. 4.6.3).

On the well-known razor from Vestrup, Jutland, safely dated to period 4, all three human figur have accentuated calves (Glob 1969, fig. 209). This dating is confirmed by the largest axe-bearer on the Vitlycke-engraving, Bohuslän (fig. 23:8), who carries a sword with a cruciform pommel and consequently should be dated to period 4.

There are a few very large (1–2 m long) hammered-out human figures in Bohuslän (Baltzer 1881–90, Pl. 3, 27:1 and 1891–1908, Pl. 2:9) which also have accentuated calves. With these overlapping can be given chronological significance and they are always found to be later than other figures. There is however no basis for the hypothesis that they are later than the end of the Bronze Age.

The miniature carving on the 10 cm long stone from Bjergagergård, Jutland (Glob 1969, fig. 105) includes a scene with a man hunting some quadrupeds (probably a deer and two hinds) with a spear. The stone was strangely enough found in a refuse pit along with sherds from about twenty pots and some flint; charcoal from this pit has been dated by C14 to 630±100 B.C. This find provides valuable confirmation that lively scenes were produced during the late phase of rock art.

13. Animals

13.1. Terminology and classification

From the source literature 2379 identifiable animal designs were recorded, making this the largest group in this study apart from the ship designs. Difficulties arise from the fact that they occur in both hunting and farming rock-engravings. We must consider whether the animal designs in these two categories are in any way connected, and if it is appropriate to include them in a single classification system. On the other hand, any attempt to create two classification systems raises the problem of how to distinguish the two categories when the areas of hunting and farming rock-engravings overlap to such an extent that the area where they coincide is larger than that where only one type occurs.

The animal designs clearly represent several different species, and this might appear to be an obvious basis for classification. However, it is often difficult, and indeed sometimes impossible, to identify the species. In considering these rock-engravings the species appears often to be decided intuitively: the general character of the whole design is first examined, then details are discovered which are thought to be typical of the particular species. Such intuitive identification is probably often correct, but in a group of figures there is always the danger that the identification of a well-drawn specimen should be extended to its perhaps more indifferently executed neighbours. As an example, it is possible to identify one of the two animals (fig. 24:6–7) from Himmelstalund, Östergötland, as a horse (fig. 24:7) and then apply the same identification to the other (fig. 24:6). But in another context, somebody else might prefer to see fig. 24:6 as a small animal, perhaps an otter. It has proved very difficult to determine clearly and unequivocally the characteristic features of different species.

It seems obvious that in these circumstances the classification system must take in the whole North European area: in so far as hunting and farming rock-engravings can be distinguished, this will have to be done in other contexts. The classification must be based not on species but on other more clearly-defined characteristics: the manner in which the body is represented, the number of legs and whether or not there are ears and/or horns or antlers. A clear division can be made between fourlegged animals (including those represented with only one foreleg and one hind leg), birds, snakes and aquatic animals (including fish, whales, porpoises and seals). It seems unreasonable, however, entirely to eschew intuitive

1 AIIc2 2 AIIn4 3 AXc4 4 BIh4

5 BIIa2 6 CIa4 7 CIh4 8 CIIh4

9 CIIn4 10 CIIs4 11 CXc4 12 DIIa4

13 DIIh2 14 DXc2 15 CF2 16 AO 17 DO

Fig. 24. Animal designs from farming rock engravings (South region). (Sites: *1:* Sporanes, Rauland, Telemark, South Norway. *2:* Aspeberget, Boshulän. *3:* Aspeberget, Bohuslän. *4:* Gladlunda, Östergötland. *5:* Lillgården, Hovås, Västergötland. *6:* Himmelstalund. Östergötland. *7:* Himmelstalund. *8:* Kivik, Scania. *9:* Aspeberget, Bohuslän. *10:* Himmelstalund, Östergötland. *11:* Leonardsberg, Östergötland. *12:* Backa in Brastad, Bohuslän. *13:* Tegneby Nordgården, Bohuslän. *14:* Fossum, Tanum, Bohuslän. *15:* Backa in Brastad, Bohuslän. *16:* Bjergagergård, Jylland, West Danmark. *17:* Aspeberget, Bohuslän.)

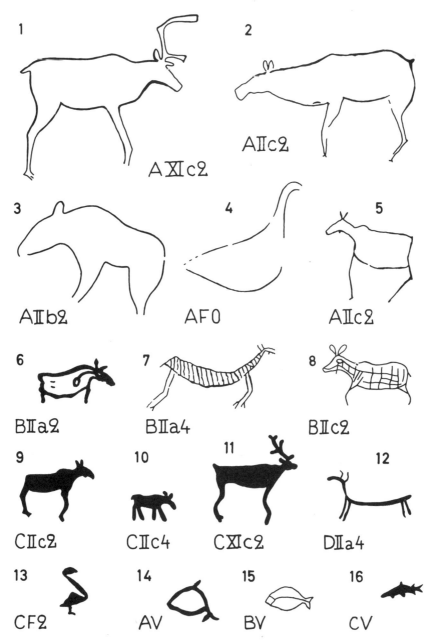

Fig. 25. Animal designs from hunting rock-engravings (North region, except 8).
(Sites: *1:* Bøla, Trøndelag. *2:* Sletjord, Nordland. *3:* Fykanvatn, Nordland. *4:* Leiknes, Nordland. *5:* Nämforsen II. Ångermanland. *6:* Nämforsen III, Ångermanland. *7:* Ausevik, Sogn og Fjordane, Middle Norway. *8:* Ekeberg, Oslo, South Norway. *9:* Nämforsen I, Ångermanland. *10:* Nämforsen II, Ångermanland. *11:* Zalavrouga, White Sea. District. *12:* Eirisfjord. Møre og Romsdal, Middle Norway. *13:* Bessov-Noss, Onega District. *14:* Kirkely, Balsfjord, Troms, North Norway. *15:* Kvernavika, Trøndelag. *16:* Nämforsen III, Ångermanland.)

identification of species. The problem may be solved by listing only those figures where the species appears evident, and assigning all other designs to a general category. It is clear, however, that intuitive identification have less value as evidence than the objectively identified elements.

It is necessary to define the following concepts:

Ears/horns or antlers may be defined thus: whenever the top of the head presents a concavity, ears, horns or antlers are said to be present; for instance fig. 24:9 but also 11 and 13. Antlers are easily distinguished (fig. 24:3, 11 and 14), but as it is not always possible to distinguish between horns and ears, these features cannot be used separately as type-defining elements. Only occasionally do ears occur along with antlers, making positive identification possible (fig. 25:1 and 11).

The *body* of the animal may be *contoured* without any lines inside the contour (fig. 24:1–3 and 25:1–5). It may be contoured with the addition of a 'life line' (fig. 24:5 and 25:6) or hatching (fig. 25:7) or other *lines within the contour* (fig. 24:4 and 25:8 and 15). The body can also be *hammered-out* (fig. 24:6–11 and 25:9–11) or a *single-line drawing* (fig. 24:12–14 and 25:12). The two last-mentioned techniques require further definition: if the widest part of the body is at least three times as thick as the centre of the widest leg, the body is deemed to be hammered-out; otherwise it is said to be drawn with a single line.

It is not usually difficult to decide whether there are two or four *legs*; but where two single lines occur at the back and at the front, it may be unclear whether two or four legs were intended (for example the engraving at Glösa, Jämtland, Hallström 1960, pl. 5–6). If two of the lines (but not the other two) meet at the foot, or if they clearly converge (fig. 25:3), the figure is said to have two legs; this is also the case if one leg is hammered-out and the other is drawn with two parallel lines. Except for these, all such animals are deemed to have four legs.

Like the quadrupeds, *birds* and *aquatic animals* can have contoured bodies with or without internal lines, can be hammered-out or singleline drawings (fig. 25:13–16). Birds may have legs (fig 24:15 and 25:13) or not (fig. 25:4).

The typological elements defined above can be expressed by means of the following twenty symbols:

A   Contoured, plain body.
B   Contoured body with internal line patterns.
C   Hammered-out body.
D   Single-line body.
F   Bird.
O   Snake.
V   Aquatic animal.
(Animals without the symbols F, O and V are quadrupeds)
 I   No ears, horns or antlers.
 II   Ears or horns.

X   Antlers, but no ears.

XI   Antlers and ears.

0   No legs.

2   (in combinations with F) one or two legs drawn.

2   (in combination with I, II, X or IX) Two legs drawn.

4   Four (or three) legs drawn.

The author's intuitive identifications of probable animal species are expressed by the following symbols:

a   Indeterminate animal species.

b   Bear.

c   Deer type (*cervidae*: deer, reindeer, elk).

h   Horse.

n   Cattle.

s   Pig.

13.2. Chorology and chronology

The source literature gives 2379 identifiable animal designs. Added to these are 36 carts (table 7) and seven ards (chapter 6) with draught animals and 45 horses with riders; there are a total of 88 such designs, of which 52 are in Bohuslän.

Animal designs are more evenly distributed over the whole North European area than any other design (table 25). Only North Germany and Bornholm have none. Richest of all is Ångermanland, where one site at Nämforsen alone accounts for 464 animal designs. Hallström (1960, p. 284) has found no less than 719 designs definitely identified as animals on this site, as well as approximately 200 uncertain designs. However, only half of these meet the criteria laid down in the present study.

In tables 25–27 the North European area has been divided into a northern and a southern region, the dividing line being the northern border of the Mälar District, West Sweden, South Norway and Rogaland (cf. the map fig. 1). There is a marked contrast between the two regions: in the south the percentage of animal to ship designs is 27.5 %; in the north 212 % (table 25, last column). These percentages may be used as a rough guide in distinguishing between hunting and farming rock-engravings. One area in the north, Trøndelag, has a proportion of only 73 %, and there is indeed a large element of farming rock-engravings in this area. In the southern region, Bohuslän (36.5 %) and Östergötland (42.5 %) have most of animal designs, and these percentages apply to a very large number of ship designs: 1155 in the former area and 645 in the latter. With 424 animal designs, Bohuslän is second only to Ångermanland.

The distribution of the animal designs is quite different from that of the motifs discussed above. The whole northern region of the area under consideration is rich in animal designs. In southern Scandinavia the distribution is more sparse but fairly even, apart from concentrations in

Bohuslän and Östergötland. It is therefore reasonable to hypothecate the existence of *two* innovation centres for animal designs, one in the north and one in the south of Scandinavia. The concentrations in Bohuslän and Östergötland could be due to influences from northern Scandinavia.

The tradition of pure hunting rock-engravings reaches far to the south, as is demonstrated by a recently-discovered rock-painting in Tumledalen, Gothenburg, West Sweden (Cullberg *et al.* 1975, p. 71). This site is to the *south* of Bohuslän, the richest area of farming rock-engravings; yet these paintings are of deer in red paint, very similar to those in Jämtland, 600 km to the north. However, the age of this painting in relation to the farming rock-engravings in the area is very uncertain.

There is more likelihood of arriving at a date for fig. 24:5, a B-type animal, that is a contoured animal with an internal pattern, a 'life line' of the kind common among the representations of animals in hunting rock-engravings (for instance fig. 25:6 from Nämforsen). But fig 24:5 comes from a rock-engraving at Hovås, Gothenburg, just south of the rockpainting in Tumledalen. The Hovås engravings include five definite ships, three foot designs, two human figures, a circular design and another animal design of type DIIa4 (Fredsjö 1956, p. 4). It is probable that all designs in this engraving are closely contemporary, including the B-type animal design. It would seem that there is no chronological reason why hunting rock-engravings may not have influenced farming rock-engravings.

The distribution of the type-defining elements can best be seen in table 27. The northern and southern regions differ greatly in the manner of drawing the animals. In the north, types A and B (contoured bodies with and without internal lines) are equally prevalent and together represent 54.5 % of quadruped design material. In the south the two types account for only 5 %. Type C (hammered-out body) occurs in about equal numbers in north and south, representing 30 to 35 % in both regions. Single-line drawings (type D) are much more common in the south (58.5 %) than in the north (14.5 %). This situation can be interpreted as implying that types A and B originated in the north and type D in the south. The opposite interpretation becomes unlikely if we postulate two innovation centres: the two regions cannot have exchanged their methods of drawing. Type C (hammered-out) perhaps provides a key to an understanding of the relationship between hunting and farming rock-engravings.

There are no great dissimilarities between south and north in the methods of representing ears, horns or antlers. Element I (no ears, horns or antlers) is, however, definitely more common in the south than in the north.

Legs are represented differently in north and south. In the south, element 4 (four legs) predominates with 72.5 %, while in the north element 2 (two legs) predominates even more exclusively with 81.5 %.

Of the species, birds (element F) are twice as common in the north as in the south, and aquatic animals (element V) are more than ten times as common in the north. On the other hand, snakes (element O) are much more common in the south.

For the quadrupeds, evidence using the relative proportions of the species is of less value, as this material is entirely based on the author's intuitive identifications. Animals of no identifiable species (element a) make up about two thirds of the whole material, rather more in the south than in the north. Bears (element b) occur only in the north and animals of deertype (element c) are more than twice as common in the north than in the south. Horses, cattle and pigs (elements h, n and s) occur only in the south.

Comparisons between the areas within the southern region are also of interest. Element A (contoured body) does not occur in Denmark and Scania. As regards the original corpus it is limited to Östergötland, West Sweden, Bohuslän och South Norway (table 25–26); according to Kjellén and Hyenstrand (1977, p. 79) it occasionally occurs in the Mälar District. B-type animals (contoured bodies with internal line patterns) are twice as common as A-type animals in the southern areas, but have an almost identical distribution, with the addition of Østfold. A and B-type animals clearly belong in the northern parts of the south region and are missing in South-East Sweden, Scania, Bornholm, West Denmark and Rogaland. In the southern region A and B-type animals have four legs more often than two, while in the north they generally have only two legs (table 25).

Hammered-out (C) and single-line (D) animal designs present a contrast: element C (hammered-out animals) predominates in Östergötland, where there are 68.5 % animal designs of this type against 28.5 % for D-type animal designs. Conversely D-type animals (drawn with a single line) predominate in Bohuslän with 85.5 % against only 13 % of C-type animal designs (table 27). West Sweden is in this regard similar to Bohuslän, and the Mälar District similar to Östergötland. There is thus a marked chorological contrast: the hammered-out C-type animal designs dominate in the east, and single-line D-type animals in the west. This presents a direct parallel with the distribution of the ship designs: the C-type hammered-out ships predominate in the east, while the single-line B-type ships predominate in the west (fig. 7–9). The comparison can be extended still further. B-type ship designs predominate over C-type ship designs in West Denmark, Østfold, South Norway and Trøndelag in the same way as D-type animal designs predominate over C-type in the same areas. Likewise C-type animal designs are more common than D-type in the eastern areas Scania, Ångermanland and Finland-Karelia.

This is of course not coincidental: the actual technique of engraving with broad hammered-out designs predominates in the east, whereas the single-line technique is the norm in west Scandinavia. Although for technical reasons the method of engraving was not included among the type-defining elements of the human figures, the same point can be applied to these designs as well. If we consider fig. 23, there is no doubt that the broad figure 23:7 comes from the east (Östergötland) as does fig. 23:6 (Scania); while the extremely thin figures 23:5 and 8 are typical of western areas (Bohuslän) as are also fig. 23:3 and 4 (West Denmark). The thinness of the western designs is to some extent compensated for by the swelling calves (fig. 23:8), a typically western stylistic trait.

The relationship between north and south must be considered further. The hypothesis which postulates an independent innovation centre for animal designs in South Scandinavia is supported by the circumstance that different species are portrayed in the two regions: in the south the domestic animals, horses, cattle and pigs, predominate slightly over wild animals like birds, aquatic animals, snakes and deer-type animals (apparently mostly red deer); in the north apparently only wild animals are portrayed, birds, aquatic animals, bears and in particular deer-type animals (apparently mainly elk and reindeer). It can however be maintained that it is no more surprising that red deer and domestic animals predominate in the southern region than that elk are depicted at Nämforsen, reindeer in North Norway and fish on the Norwegian coast. In addition, while the horse is relatively best represented in Scania and South-East Sweden, cattle and pigs do not occur at all in the far south, but only in Östergötland, the Mälar District and Bohuslän. Moreover, the identification of the animal on the design from Bohuslän (fig. 24:9) as a bull is open to question; the animal may equally well be a hunted beast, an aurochs. The pigs portrayed in Östergötland and the Mälar District (fig. 24:10) have large snouts, which rather suggest a wild breed. These animals may be seen as a manifestation of the northern tradition of depicting hunted animals, although here the hunted breeds are those of immediate concern to hunters in Central Sweden.

It would seem that the birds also represent a northern trait in the south. They occur, although sparingly, in most northern areas—and are very numerous in the Onega District—but in the southern region they occur only in its northern areas, in Bohuslän and occasionally in South Norway, Östergötland and the Mälar District (Kjellén and Hyenstrand 1977, p. 80).

The deer-type animal designs (element c, table 26) are also typically found in the northern part of the southern region: South Norway, Østfold, Bohuslän and Östergötland. Added to these are the deer at Sagaholm, which formally belongs to South-East Sweden, but is situated just south-west of the border with Östergötland. The three deer designs in Denmark are all from the miniature engraving from Bjergagergård, Jutland (Glob 1969, fig. 105); this lively hunting scene has given rise to the hypothesis that the stone could possibly have been imported from Bohuslän (12.2).

The Sagaholm find is the most important reference for dating the postulated influence of the North Scandinavian hunting rock-engravings on the South Scandinavian farming rock-engravings: deer and horses, with legs characteristically pointing forward (fig. 15), occur together with ship designs of type C. The grave mound undoubtedly belongs to the local Early Bronze Age. Elements from hunting rock-engravings seem to have been adopted into farming rock-engravings at the same time, or very shortly after these were first introduced in Östergötland.

The forward-pointing legs are characteristic of animal design in the southern region and occur already in the bronze horses from Trundholm, period 2 (Broholm 1952 B, fig. 199) and Tågaborg (Montelius 1917, fig. 980). This stance is seen in a fully developed and stylised form in the quadrupeds on stone 3 at Kivik, which has been defined as type CIIh4 (fig. 6:3, cf. fig. 24:8). They have been identified as horses, and, if they are compared with the draught horses on stone 7, this seems the only possible interpretation. Apart from the forward-pointing legs, another characteristic difference is that animal designs in the southern region usually have four legs, while in the north an even larger proportion of animals have only two (Table 27). This difference, together with the fact that horse designs occurred as early as period 2 in South Scandinavia, indicates that animal designs were certainly included in farming rock-engravings from the start.

In conclusion, therefore, it is possible to risk formulating the hypothesis that, apart from the main area of animal designs in the north, another innovation centre existed in South Scandinavia, probably already in period 2, consisting of Scania and probably Denmark as well. Only one animal species, the horse, was portrayed; the greater variety of species which began to appear shortly afterwards in Bohuslän and Östergötland was the result of influences from hunting rock-engravings.

Apart from the horse, only one other animal, the snake, is really typical of the southern region. It is seen on the famous razor from Vestrup in period 4 (Glob 1969, p. 190, fig. 209) and on the miniature engraving from Bergagergård (fig. 24:16, cf. Glob 1969, fig. 105), dated by C14 to the end of the Bronze Age. The representations of snakes seem therefore to belong to the Late Bronze Age. Geographically they have a western orientation, concentrated in Scania, West Sweden and Bohuslän with occasional examples in adjacent areas.

13.3. Animal designs at Nämforsen

The rock-engravings at Nämforsen in Ångermanland hold a key position in North European rock art, not least in any assessment of the relationship between North and South Scandinavian engravings.

The rock-engravings at Nämforsen cover a wide area almost 500 m in length along the river Ångermanälven. The distances between individual engravings can be as great as 100 m, although in such cases the distance usually includes water crossings. It is clear, however, that these engravings form a well-defined unit. The distance to the nearest known engravings to the west, Fångsjön in Jämtland, is 60 km, and to the east, Åbosjön in eastern Ångermanland, 70 km. The nearest rock art site to the north is the recently-discovered rock-painting at Sämsjön, Åsele parish, Lappland (the first rock art site to be identified in North Norrland), 80 km from Nämforsen. To the south the nearest known rock-engravings are 400 km away in the Mälar District.

Following Hallström (1960, p. 139 and 283), the Nämforsen site has been divided into three sections, I–III (see map fig. 26). Nämforsen II is to the east and consists of the rocky island Notön (with the adjacent gravel bank Ören down stream). Nämforsen III is the central island of Brådön. Nämforsen I is a topographically less uniform area comprising scattered rock-engravings on the south and north banks of the river, especially on the so-called Laxön; this was not an island in prehistoric times, but was created recently by blasting a channel. Notön (II) and Brådön (III) are, however, true islands separated from the banks by running water 40 m wide at its narrowest point. Before the building of the hydro-electric power station it was relatively difficult to reach these islands: the total fall is 22.5 m and the maximum flow of water 2900 m^3 per second (Hallström 1960, p. 128).

The Nämforsen site has a total of 1742 designs (plus a large number of incomplete or partly obliterated designs); 567 of these are in Nämforsen I (the river banks), 795 in Nämforsen II (Notön) and 380 in Nämforsen III (Brådön). The number of animal designs identified according to the conditions laid down in the present study is 464; of these 176 are in Nämforsen I, 146 in Nämforsen II and 142 in Nämforsen III (table 28).

The first question which arises from the rock-engravings at Nämforsen is the sequence in which they were produced. Did engraving take place over the entire 500 m-long stretch from the beginning, or did it originate at a certain location on the banks of the river or perhaps on one of the islands?

Initially a chorological study can be undertaken comparing the contoured designs of A and B-type with those of the hammered-out C-type. Are these equally represented in the three sections Nämforsen I, II and III?

Hallström sees the hammered-out animal designs of C-type as a late innovation in hunting rock-engravings. On the Nämforsen site, however, he considers it likely that they are contemporary with the A and B-type animal designs. He makes an exception for A and B-type animals of particularly large size, which he believes to be earlier and associated with

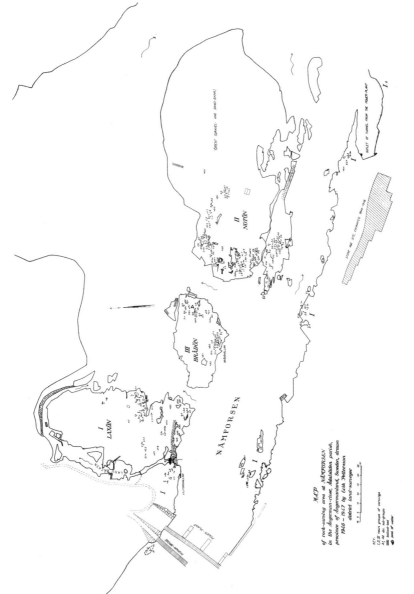

Fig. 26. Map of the rock-engraving area at Nämforsen. (After Hallström 1960.)

the large contoured animal designs in North Norway and Trøndelag, although these are more naturalistic (fig. 25: 1–3). Hallström identifies examples of these large contoured animal designs (for example fig. 25: 5) in all three sections of Nämforsen (Hallström 1960, p. 287). This implies that engravings were carried out at several different points along the 500 m-long Nämforsen site from the beginning. But this assertion is not sufficient. It is still possible that, relatively speaking, A, B and C-type animals are not equally represented in the three sections, from which we could conclude that engravings were not continually produced with the same intensity over the entire area, but that one part of it was preferred to another at various times.

Tables 29–30 show that the proportion of A, B and C-type animal designs clearly differs between the sections. The relative frequency of A-type animals is greatest on the central Brådön (Nämforsen III) with 51.5 % (this is also true of the actual numbers of such designs: there are 71 examples, cf. table 29). Notön (II) has 43 % and the river banks (I) 24.5 %. Similarly, the B-type designs occur most frequently on Brådön (III) with 24 %, followed by Notön (II) with 7 % and lastly the river banks (I) with 2.5 %.

The hammered-out C-type designs present a reversal of this series: the river banks (I) lead with 72.5 % (also in actual numbers, with 161 examples), followed by Notön (II) with 43 % and lastly Brådön (III) with 24.5 %. Single-line animal designs of type D occur almost exclusively on Notön (II) where they represent only 7 %.

These differences cannot be coincidental. An obvious hypothesis is that while engravings were carried out continually over the whole area, the islands in the river, Brådön (III) and Notön (II), were at first definitely preferred. Towards the end of the period when engravings were produced, more designs were placed on the river banks (I) than on the inaccessible islands. This presupposes that the C-type animal designs are in fact later than those of type A and B. In any case, the different distributions in the three sections demonstrate that there is a *time difference* between types A and B and type C. That type C is in fact peculiar to Nämforsen indicates that it is the later form. C-type designs are poorly represented in the adjacent areas of the Scandinavian peninsula. Curiously, a similar preference for hammered-out C-type animal designs is found only in the Onega and White Sea Districts.

Since the hammered-out C-type animal designs in South Scandinavia are of an early date—they are represented in Kivik—and since they have a very uneven distribution among North Scandinavian hunting rock-engravings, another hypothesis naturally follows: it is possible that the technique of hammering-out designs at Nämforsen was the result of southern influences, presumably from Östergötland and the Mälar District, where this technique is more common than elsewhere in South

Scandinavia. The obvious weakness of this argument is the relatively modest character of this innovation, which could easily have arisen spontaneously.

In order to test the hypotheses made here it is necessary to examine the distribution of more definitely southern traits in Nämforsen I, II and III. An examination of this kind was made in the chapter on ship designs above (4.7). Unlike the animal designs, ship designs were found to be very unevenly distributed: Brådön (III) had only 16 ship designs as against Notön (II) with 139 and the river banks (I) with 65 ship designs (table 6). It was nevertheless on Brådön (III) that almost all the early ship designs were recorded, 6 examples of AI and AII-type ships. There was only one AI-type ship design on Notön (II) and no early designs on the river banks (I).

The great majority of ship designs at Nämforsen are AIII-type, particularly type AIIIc1, a double-line ship without crew or ribs, with two single prows, usually with an animal head at the stem; AIIIa1, a similar ship with crew lines (Hallström 1960, pl. 14:G: 6); and AIIIa2, a similar ship with both ribs and crew lines. These are what are usually called Stone Age boats (Gjessing 1936, p. 85; Bakka 1975, p. 120). B-type, single-line ships, are less common at Nämforsen. It is noteworthy, however, that B-type ships (Hallström 1960, pl. 13) make up 31 % of the total number on the river banks (I), but only 5 % on Notön (II) and 19 % on Brådön (III).

In conclusion we find that the early type AI and AII ship designs occur only on Brådön and Notön, and that type B ships are considerably more common on the river banks (I) than on the islands (II and III). The presence of AI and AII ship designs of South Scandinavian type on Brådön and Notön (III and II), where early animal designs predominate, supports the hypothesis that the 'Stone Age boats' of AIII type are in fact modifications of the AIa1 ship designs of the farming rock-engravings of Rørby type, represented by one damaged example on Notön (Hallström 1960, pl. 18: G:1); many factors mentioned in this study also suggest that this type spread rapidly northwards. Evidently this hypothesis does not preclude the possibility that in certain details the AIII designs may portray boats in use on the river Ångermanälven; 366 ship or boat designs (of which 220 are identified according to the conditions laid down in this study) suggest a considerable interest in boat-building and seafaring, in particular as the designs are if anything more realistic than those of South Scandinavia.

The foot designs are also of interest; there are 18 at Nämforsen, if pairs are counted as one figure, and 28 if each foot is taken separately (table 16). All are contoured shoe designs (B2). 19 designs have cross-straps (element b) and 9 are without (element a). The chronological discussion in chapter 10 gave the following results: the type A design (naked foot) is much later than the shod foot and appears in the transition between periods 3 and 4. The type B foot design first appears in periods 2–3, but later than the earliest ship designs. Type B shoe designs (shod foot) tend to occur in pairs twice as often as type A. Earliest is B2, the contoured shoe design, at first usually with a cross-strap (Bb2), which therefore is particularly common in northern areas, peripheral to Denmark.

All feet at Nämforsen are of type B2, and two thirds of these are of type Bb2. The tendency to occur in pairs is 71.5 % at Nämforsen (table 13), one of the highest percentages for any area. The foot designs at Nämforsen are thus of the earliest type.

The distribution of foot designs between the different sections of the Nämforsen site is as follows: 22 single designs are on Brådön (III), 3 on Notön (II) and 3 on the river banks (I). Once more we find that a definitely early, southern trait, like the B2 foot designs, is by far best represented on the islands, where the earliest animal designs also predominate (contoured type A and B designs).

There are also two circular designs on the Nämforsen site. Both are of the earliest type, Aa1 (cf. 11.4 and table 17), a circle with four radii; one is on Brådön (III) and the other on the river banks (I). The earliest type of circular design therefore followed the earliest ship designs and the earliest shoe design by a very rapid innovation process from South Scandinavia to Nämforsen. The ship design was thoroughly assimilated and apparently transformed to portray the type of boat used locally; the engraving of foot designs continued for a while unchanged, while the circular designs won no popularity at Nämforsen. This is perhaps an indication that it does not symbolise the sun, but rather the wheel, a motif of little immediate appeal in Ångermanland.

With regard to the human figure, only one feature of chronological importance may be discerned at Nämforsen. While most are hammered-out and relatively slim (fig. 18:7), a minority have wide contoured trunks, described by Hallström as 'triangular' (1960, p. 317). These contoured human figures occur only on Brådön (III) and Notön (II), that is, in those sections where the contoured type A and B animal designs are in the majority. It is thus possible to hypothecate that the contoured human figures are the earliest at Nämforsen; further, and no less importantly—that in the earliest phase of hunting rock-engravings, before this area was reached by influences from farming rock-engravings, their motifs included not only animal designs but human figures as well.

By what route did the southern influences reach Nämforsen? By a western route from Norway, probably by way of Trøndelag, or by a southern route along the coast from Östergötland and the Mälar District? If there is any connection between type C animals at Nämforsen and similar designs in South Scandinavia, the influence must have come from the south, as it is in Östergötland and the Mälar District that C-type animals are best represented, while there is only a negligible proportion of such designs in Trøndelag and North Norway (table 27). The other southern features at Nämforsen also have clear parallels in Östergötland and the Mälar District. The A-type ship designs are well represented in these areas (especially in their original form AIa1, which occurs at Nämforsen). The foot design types which occur at Nämforsen (BIa2, BIIa2, BIb2, and BIIb2, table 16) represent 89 % of the foot designs in Östergötland (table 11) and 76 % in Uppland (from the control corpus) while a further 22 % are of the closely-related type BIIa1.

The circular designs are perhaps even more significant. While A-type ship designs and B-type foot designs occur only slightly less frequently in Trøndelag and North Norway than in Östergötland and the Mälar District, the proportion of circular design Ala is 55 % in Östergötland, 43.5 % in the Mälar District, 8 % in Trøndelag and 16.5 % in Hordaland (table 17 and control corpus, not listed in the table).

Another possibility is being given consideration by other scholars: a connection eastwards between Nämforsen and Karelia, the Onega and White Sea Districts, where hammered-out, naturalistic C-type animal designs predominate to a larger extent than in any other area (table 27), being stylistically very similar to the Nämforsen designs, although usually of larger size.

Recently published C14 datings from the White Sea District suggest that these engravings are very old. An occupation layer at a settlement in Besovy Sledki is dated to 5430±50BP; for no other reason than that the rock-engravings are rather near, it is thought that they were produced by the inhabitants of this settlement (Savvateev 1968, p. 150; Bakka 1975, p. 118). The find does not actually prove the connection: more weight should apparently be given to the dating from Zalavruga I. The excavation report published by Savvateev (1968, p. 149) reads: "After a couple of hundred years, probably in connection with the White Sea's transgression, the water level of the mouth of the Vyg rose and for some time the rock-engravings were under water, and covered by a sand-bank approximately one metre high. At the end of the second millenium before our era Zalavruga merged from the waters and was settled. The settlement can be dated with certainty to the end of the second millenium before our era... To determine the date of the settlement in Zalavruga I the C14 method has been used. Charcoal from the settlement's fire place has been examined... It has been established that the date of the settlement was 4010±70 years... One may imagine that this fire was built before the site was settled (it was in fact found below the occupation layer) and left untouched by the artists responsible for the rock-engravings." This excavation report contains some contradictions: the rock-engravings are said to have been found *under* the sand deposit *on top* of which the settlement inhabitated by the artists was established. There are, above all, no plans or sections. Without them, the possibility cannot be excluded that Neolithic remains were redeposited on top of rock-engravings from the Bronze Age, particularly as this site is a river mouth with sand-banks.

In the present study it has been observed many times that the Karelian rock-engravings differ from those of Scandinavia, despite the obvious similarities, especially in ship and animal designs, and particularly between Karelia and Nämforsen. Chorological and comparative studies have produced no definite conclusions about the relationship between Karelian and Scandinavian rock-engravings. A solution may perhaps be reached by other methods, but further consideration is outside the framework of the present study.

13.4. The relationship between rock-engravings of animals in north and south

Animal designs appear in South Scandinavia perhaps as early as period 2, and are definitely recorded in the Kivik cist from the beginning of period 3, where they take the form of hammered-out designs of moderate width probably representing horses. As the animal designs spread northwards they begin to separate into two distinct styles, a division also observed in other rock art motifs: a single-line style (D-type animals) in Bohuslän and the rest of West Scandinavia, and a broad hammered-out style (C-type animals) in the east. Contoured B- and A-type animal designs (with and without 'life lines' and other internal line patterns) occur only north of Denmark and Scania. They may be seen as influenced by hunting rock-engravings, particularly as a rock-painting of a B-type animal design with 'life line' has been found as far south as Gothenburg. Another influence from hunting rock-engravings is perhaps the richness of the fauna portrayed in the rock-engravings at Bohuslän, Östergötland and the Mälar District by comparison with Denmark and Scania. One can identify all animals which occur on farming rock-engravings as hunted animals apart from the specifically southern motifs, the horse and the snake.

The argument above presupposes that there were already hunting rock-engravings in Norway and in North and Central Sweden as far south as Gothenburg when the farming rock-engravings reached these areas fairly early in the Early Bronze Age. This implies that some hunting rock-engravings belong to the Neolithic. The rock-engravings with animal designs in the north are relatively rare (about 700 examples apart from those at Nämforsen and in Karelia); this should serve as a warning not to allot them too long a period of existence. The majority, and perhaps all, probably belong to the late Middle Neolithic or the Late Neolithic.

The innovation centre for the northern animal engravings is presumably North Norway, and perhaps Nordland in particular. The earliest type is presumably a naturalistic contoured animal (type A) of large size. The custom of engraving spread southwards, while at the same time the style successively changed to the B-type animal design (internal line pattern), schematic drawing, painting instead of engraving, a smaller size and the creation of multiple engravings in large groups. It is possible that the small size and the multiple engravings were influenced, or perhaps initiated, by contact with farming rock-engravings, as is suggested at Nämforsen: on Notön (II) and Brådön (III), small type A and B animal designs occur together with clearly southern motifs from the repertoire of farming rock-engravings. At a certain time, probably during the early Late Bronze Age, there is a radical change in style, which is particularly noticeable at Nämforsen I (the river banks), where hammered-out, fairly naturalistic C-type animals appear. This can probably be associated with the preférence for type C animal designs in eastern South Scandinavia (Östergötland and the Mälar District), and perhaps also in Karelia.

In conclusion it may be stated that the richness of Scandinavian rock art depended on Continental impulses arriving by way of Denmark and Scania. The exceptional profusion in Bohuslän and Östergötland, and to some extent in the Mälar District, would have resulted from the existence of a living rock art tradition of the Neolithic, which in these areas received the impulses from the south. The same explanation may apply to Nämforsen and perhaps also to Karelia.

14. Summary and final discussion

14.1. Point of departure

The most important aspect of rock art is its *meaning*. All other kinds of archaeological material have at least *some* practical purpose. The settlement serves the living, the graves the dead. The tool must be able to perform its practical task, the weapon be fit for hunting or battle. The field provides subsistence, the ship transport. All artefacts and monuments have been influenced to some degree by ideas of status, solidarity within the community, beauty, magic or religion. We may approach these aspects of the material by making simple calculations regarding the size of the artefact, the scarcity of the material or the quality of the work. In the main, such aspects fail us in rock art. This is a *message* from the prehistoric artist (and/or his patron) to mankind (including ourselves) or to certain particular people: in both cases probably at the same time also to higher powers.

We will never be able completely to understand the meaning of rock art. *If* it were possible to interpret its significance, it is beyond doubt that this could be expressed in words. Rather than speaking of *rock art* we should say *rock language*. The aesthetic aspect is more an expression of our relationship to rock art than our relationship to prehistoric man.

Even if one did not understand a word of a certain language, it could still be used for cultural and social studies. It is not necessary to take so obvious an example as hieroglyphics: without being deciphered they would still provide an exceptionally clear conception of the extent and intensity of ancient Egyptian culture. We may equally well take Hungarian as an example: without any interpretation or understanding of the language, dated texts in Hungarian would still convey to us something important about cultural and social conditions in the Danube basin. Such chorological studies of a (postulated) dead language would actually tell us more than comparable studies of, say, Spondylus shells or Roman *denarii* (that is not to say that these do not deserve study). Language is a more genuine expression of people and their society than any imported objects that may be found.

An axe, or any kind of artefact, can be interpreted in isolation, because its form and function are so simple that it can be understood by reference to the modern observer's own experience. It can of course be better understood if all examples of a type can be studied, providing information about the full range of shapes, sizes and contexts. This complete picture is *necessary* in the study of so complex a phenomenon as rock art. An isolated rock surface covered with engravings inspires in the modern observer so many associations of ideas that he finds it difficult to distinguish matters of primary and secondary importance (apart from the strong possibility that his ideas are inadequate and that he has missed the central point of the engraving's significance).

The present study is based on the conviction that in order to interpret rock art it is necessary to survey the whole body of material and its variations in space, time and context. The exposition concentrates on the chorological aspect because a large amount of unexploited material was available. A number of regional collections of material have been published which bear witness to considerable diligence and application, covering at least the majority of the North European rock art areas. There has been less interest in making a survey of the whole of this area: it is the aim of the present study to try and fill this gap to some extent.

14.2. Results

The differences between the geographical areas with regard to the quantity and quality of rock art motifs are not arbitrary: seen as a whole they show that the innovation process of the farming rock-engravings began in the south, in Denmark and Scania, whence it gradually reached the northernmost part of the area under consideration, Troms-Finnmark. It is possible that these impulses also reached Karelia, but this is difficult to prove because the Scandinavian and Karelian areas which have rock-engravings are separated by the quite distinct rock-painting area of Finland.

It is likely that the innovation centre for the hunting rock-engravings lay in Norwegian Nordland. In any case, the innovation of farming rock-engravings encountered, as it spread northwards, an existing tradition of hunting rock-engravings in a wide zone, and primarily in Nämforsen, the Mälar District, Östergötland and Bohuslän (possibly also Karelia). Seen in the context of Europe as a whole, the exceptional vitality of the rock art of Bohuslän, Östergötland and the Mälar District, as well as of Nämforsen, may be explained by this combination of two traditions of rock-engraving.

In Norway, areas rich in farming rock-engravings are generally also the areas with the best agricultural land: Østfold, Rogaland and Trøndelag. Of the best agricultural areas in South Scandinavia, only the Mälar District and Östergötland are very rich in farming rock-engravings. North Germany, West Denmark, Scania, Halland and Västergötland have remarkably few such rock-engravings, considering the extent of good farming land and the substantial quantities of bronze which have been recovered from these areas. The comparative lack of interest in farming rock-engravings in so rich an agricultural area is a phenomenon of the south-west. In other words, rock art is peripheral to the economic and material centre of Bronze Age culture.

The south-north innovation pattern of the farming rock-engravings varies with regard to the different motifs, and indeed also to the various types within the motifs. However, a contrast between east and west is a constant feature. In a number of motifs (ships, human figures and animals) a broad, hammered-out style is characteristic of the eastern areas, and a thin single-line style of the west. This contrast may be due to more important lines of communication running north-south by comparison with those running east-west. We can therefore distinguish two routes along which the innovations emanating from West Denmark spread. The principal areas of the eastern route are Östergötland and the Mälar District, and at a later stage also Ångermanland. The principal areas of the western route are Bohuslän, Østfold, Rogaland and Trøndelag. The position of Scania is somewhat ambivalent, as it is variously linked with both the eastern and the western routes. By comparison with West Denmark, the primary centre of diffusion, Scania always appears to be clearly of the east, while Denmark itself has far stronger affinities with the western areas. The islands of Bornholm, Öland and Gotland may be regarded as composing a separate diffusion route, which in some respects included Blekinge and Småland (that is, the whole of Småland except Sagaholm in the north, which is linked with Östergötland). North Germany may belong to the primary diffusion centre in West Denmark, but appears in some respects to be secondary to it.

Another chorological grouping which partly coincides with the routes here identified is of a more static character. In the central area of West Denmark, most interest is shown in abstract and symbolic designs: circular designs, hands and feet. Immediately to the east of West Denmark, mainly in Bohuslän, but also in Østfold, West Sweden and Scania, there is a pronounced interest in scenes: the human figure in action—acrobats for example—ships' crews drawn in full, carts, ards and hunting scenes. This may be explained by postulating that cultic ceremonies performed in West Denmark, and well-known in these areas, were here portrayed in stone as there was less opportunity to practise them in real life. In an outer zone around West Denmark (comprising principally Östergötland and the Mälar District, but also to some extent Scania) scenes are less common, but full-scale representations of weapons and clothing do occur. One may hypothecate that the myths and cultic ceremonies of the central Danish areas were less well known in these eastern areas; instead we find portrayals of the sacrifices which were deposited in kind in West Denmark and the immediate vicinity, and Scania in particular.

A third chorological grouping has been distinguished: there are further innovation centres other than West Denmark, in particular Scania, Östergötland, Bohuslän, Østfold, Rogaland and Trøndelag. The intermediate, larger areas are secondary, receiving innovations later and apparently by way of these other innovation centres. Typical of areas with a secondary diffusion pattern for farming rock-engravings are South-East Sweden, West Sweden, South Norway, Middle Norway and North Norway. Nordland, which is included in the last-mentioned area, is, however, probably the innovation centre for hunting rock-engravings.

Knowledge of rock art motifs did of course spread mainly through personal contact. We may assume that bronze sculptures like the Trundholm cart and the Fårdal group contributed to this, along with engraved designs on razors such as ships and related motifs. This is how we must interpret also the beginnings of farming rock-engravings in Sweden; imported designs from the south must have played a part. The design of a chariot on stone no. 7 at Kivik (fig. 16:1) must ultimately be Mediterranean in origin. The imported designs may not have been in bronze—textiles are another possible medium, suggested by the rectangular frames around the designs on the Kivik stones (fig. 6). These frames seem unnecessary, as the carefully dressed edges of the rectangular stone would seem to provide satisfactory frames. They can, however, be interpreted as the borders of cloth with woven, applied or embroidered pictures, cloth which may have decorated the walls of a room or grave. Indeed, there appears to be a rudimentary frame of this kind on one of the stones at Sagaholm (fig. 15:6, left), which is closely related to the Kivik cist. No imported textiles have been found from the Scandinavian Bronze Age. However, the clothing which was found in the oak-log graves can best be explained as of Mediterranean inspiration: the cloak, tunic and the cap, which seems to be designed to protect against excessive heat rather than cold.

14.3. Economic aspects

Rock art does not of course simply follow on from the presence of imported designs. The North European farming rock-engravings are as much an independent Scandinavian creation as Scandinavian Bronze Age culture as a whole. The unique quality of this culture within the European Bronze Age cultures has perhaps not been sufficiently emphasised in the literature. Unlike the Continent and the the British Isles, Bronze Age Scandinavia had no exploitable resources of copper, tin, zinc and gold. This must have resulted in certain peculiarly Scandinavian economic and social phenomena: more than elsewhere in

Europe, the manufacture and use of gold and bronze objects was the prerogative of landowners in the richest agricultural areas, mainly Denmark and Scania and, although relatively less rich, Östergötland, the Mälar District, Østfold, Rogaland and Trøndelag.

It seems natural to view rock art motifs in this light. Features signifying wealth and status are emphasised: axes, swords, spears, and bronze shields; shoes, tunics and cloaks of a kind which could not have been owned by the common people. Carts were portrayed, and wheel-crosses representing the most extraordinary feature of these carts: the wheels themselves. Also horses, but not cattle or sheep, which must have been of great importance to the economy of the common people: only horses, with their considerable status value. Ploughing, which must also have been of immediate interest to most people, was rarely shown, and was always accompanied by magic and ritual features. Ceremonies were portrayed, processions with axes or shields, according well with the general pattern. The foot designs may indeed represent an invisible god, although the evidence for this is taken from far distant times and places (Almgren 1962). The very concept of an *invisible* god seems a little strange in the context of the robust symbols of the farming rock-engravings. And the variable sizes of the engraved human figures could rather lead to the hypothesis that some of them were gods. An alternative hypothesis interprets the foot designs as a symbol of the self, the human presence and perhaps the right of ownership (Kjellén and Hyenstrand 1977). It is generally possible to see the rock-engravings as territorial markers, indicative of the rights of possession: this has often been suggested in connection with grave mounds and cairns.

There is no doubt that possible prototypes for the Scandinavian rock art ship may be found in the Mediterranean (cf. Kjellén and Hyenstrand, p. 63, fig. 51), but why then was this motif adopted in Scandinavia? It is of course possible that the ship symbolises an aniconic god, but it could symbolise almost anything. The movement of the sun across the sky, the journey of the dead to another world, water, power over the water, cooperation: the possibilities are almost inexhaustible. Such interpretations are valid at all times and in all countries; specific to the Scandinavian Bronze Age is the fact that all bronze would have to be imported and that all imports came by boat. Starting with this fact of fundamental importance to Scandinavian Bronze Age culture, the ship may subsequently have taken on any other symbolic significance from the numerous possibilities it offers.

The all-important problem which eventually arises from almost any inquiry into the Scandinavian Bronze Age is this: how was the imported metal paid for? The fact that most bronze is found in the best agricultural areas must not lead one to the conclusion that the metal was paid for with agricultural produce. Such exports would be unlikely, given that the countries exporting the metal were much stronger agriculturally than Scandinavia.

One possibility is that the export was of furs. It can be maintained that such exports would only have been of marginal importance. Against this it can be argued that the importation of bronze and the bronze trade was also of secondary importance by comparison with the predominant farming economy. Bronzes, not furs, have been preserved to the present day; perhaps this is the only difference.

This hypothesis is supported by the evidence of a South Scandinavian Bronze Age culture in the northern part of Fennoscandia where the fur trade must have had its origins: there are Bronze Age cairns along the coasts of Swedish Norrland (Baudou 1968) and Finland (Meinander 1954 B). Considerable numbers of South Scandinavian bronzes have been found in Finland, even as far away as Savolaks and south Karelia, not least the hoard in Sodankylä in Finnish Lappland which contains four South Scandinavian bronze swords (Meinander 1954 B, pp. 210–230, Abb. 37, Taf. 4c, 9h and 16). Along with this evidence of South Scandinavian Bronze Age culture in the north, one must also consider the significant South Scandinavian features of the Nämforsen rock-engravings. Nämforsen would have been suitable in every respect as a meeting place for the hunters of the north and the southern traders. The fact that the profits from this trade, the bronzes, remained in areas with a strong economy—Denmark and Scania—is not exceptional in economic history: indeed, it is typical.

A few more words may be added on the chorological variations of motifs.

When the ship motif first appears it is highly stylised (AIa1): this does not have the appearance of an artist's first attempts at portraying a ship. It is more likely to be a copy of an imported ship motif (and an imported concept). The ship motif then develops in two directions: many unrelated ornaments and decorations are added, which may indicate that its symbolic significance remained unchanged, while real ships were uncommon in the area; in other areas the ship design becomes more realistic, which may indicate that it took on some other symbolic significance. The realistic ship designs belong to areas in the north: the Mälar District, Nämforsen and Karelia. It seems reasonable to suppose that the boats portrayed at Nämforsen were in fact those in use on the river.

The frequency of the ship designs is not unconnected with the importance of sea transport in the various areas. Of 72 ship designs from Denmark, 46 are from Bornholm and 22 from the western islands, while Jutland, being part of the continental land mass, has only 4, although it forms two thirds of Denmark's surface area; there are none in North Germany. Rogaland is one of the vigorous innovation centres in Northern Europe: situated at Norway's south-westernmost point, it depends almost entirely on sea transport for its imports. In Rogaland the ship designs comprise 72 % of the total number of figures, the largest percentage of ship designs recorded in any area.

The two-wheeled chariot is a natural symbol of the warrior and ruling classes. It is doubtful that real chariots were ever seen in Northern Europe during the Bronze Age; it is certainly clear that the earliest, and definitely the best executed, variant of this motif, A1a (fig. 16:1), was probably a copy of an imported design. The fact that real carts did not occur, or were at least rare, outside Denmark explains why the cart motif never become popular. It also provides an explanation for its probable transformation into a ploughing scene (fig. 17), an image all could understand. With this transformation the symbolic significance also substantially changes, presumably from the concept of power-wealth-happiness to fertility-wealth-happiness. It is above all in the rock art area of Bohuslän that the creative power to transform and change motifs is found. One can point to its position between four rich agricultural areas, Denmark, Västergötland, Halland and Østfold, and to the ready availability of suitable rock surfaces, but the ultimate reason is irrational; as irrational as the presence of two thirds of all Swedish passage-graves on the Cambro-Silurian area in Västergötland, an area representing only 0.3 % of Sweden's total area. It just happened that way.

The circular designs in Denmark are usually of type A1a, a circle with four radii; this was perhaps an example of *pars pro toto*, the wheels of the chariot instead of the whole vehicle. In northern areas, where circular designs take on a large variety of different and irregular shapes (fig. 22), there is perhaps a shift in its significance, from representing the warrior and ruling class to a more general protective and lucky sign.

The only animal portrayed in the Early Bronze Age in Scania (and Denmark) is the horse, which naturally can be interpreted as the symbol of a warrior and ruling class. As the animal motif spread northwards many different species of hunted animals began to be portrayed, and again we can probably note a shift in significance, from the concepts of power and wealth to fertility and subsistence.

14.4. Approaches to interpretation

A distinction may be made between *absolute interpretation* and *relative interpretation*. Although never found in a pure form, these two concepts can be seen as polarising present scholarship on the meaning of rock art.

Absolute interpretations look immediately to the central significance of the symbol. If in Buddhist India at the beginning of our era a pair of foot soles represent the divinity, the motif is given the same interpretation in Scandinavia a thousand years earlier. If a ship represents the actual divinity among Tacitus' *Suebi* and also in a carnival in Flanders in the year 1133 AD, the meaning should have been the same in the Scandinavian Bronze Age (Almgren 1962). For absolute interpretations, chronological and chorological facts are secondary. It is believed that a fundamental significance has been discerned, broadly human and universal, valid at least for a large span in time and space. Other possible interpretations of the significance of, for instance, the foot motif (Mandt 1972, p. 131), are rejected implicitly as of secondary or negligible importance.

Relative interpretations reject the possibility of arriving immediately at an understanding of the central symbolic significance of a motif, either by means of intuition or on the basis of material compiled from the realms of ethnography and religious history. The material available for study according to this persuasion is first of all the *variations* of a motif, both geographical and chronological. The major characteristics of a motif are illuminated through its variations and enable us to pronounce with some certainty on the objects represented, and indeed to decide whether or not a representation was in fact intended. It is through these variations and the manner in which an object is portrayed that we may learn something of the ideas with which is was associated.

Interpretations within the spheres of myths and gods, cult and religion lie outside the scope of this study. But our final conclusion must be, that future research on Scandinavian rock art and its meaning both could and should concentrate in the first instance on the contemporary cultural context in which it was produced.

Tables

Table 1 A. Ship designs by type and area.

Area	AIaI	2	3	AIbI	2	3	AIcI	2	3	AIIaI	2	AIIbI	2	3	AIIcI	2	3	AIIIaI	2	AIIIbI	2	3	AIIIcI	2	3
(2a) West Denmark	3	–	–	–	–	–	–	–	–	–	–	–	–	–	–	–	–	–	–	–	–	–	–	–	–
(2b) Bornholm	1	1	–	3	–	–	5	23	–	–	–	–	–	–	–	–	–	–	–	–	–	–	–	–	–
(2) Denmark	4	1	–	3	–	–	5	23	–	–	–	–	–	–	–	–	–	–	–	–	–	–	–	1	–
(3) Scania	42	–	1	1	–	–	12	–	–	–	–	2	–	–	–	–	1	–	–	–	–	–	–	–	–
(4) South-East Sweden	24	8	–	2	2	–	1	1	–	16	6	–	–	–	–	–	–	–	–	–	–	–	–	–	–
(5) Östergötland	98	63	17	12	4	11	69	28	2	1	–	–	–	–	17	–	–	5	–	–	–	–	9	–	–
(6) Mälar District	65	6	1	–	–	–	6	4	8	–	–	–	–	–	4	–	–	–	–	–	–	–	1	–	–
(9) Ångermanland	1	1	–	–	–	–	–	1	–	1	–	–	–	–	–	–	–	20	19	4	4	1	102	29	–
(11) West Sweden	–	1	–	4	2	–	–	–	–	–	–	–	4	–	–	–	–	–	–	–	–	–	–	–	–
(12) Bohuslän	80	102	5	36	48	1	64	28	5	7	2	5	–	–	3	6	–	1	2	1	1	–	2	–	–
(13) Østfold	58	30	1	11	5	–	7	2	–	1	4	1	–	–	6	1	1	–	–	–	–	–	–	–	–
(14) South Norway	34	7	–	6	3	–	14	2	–	2	1	–	–	1	–	3	–	–	1	–	–	–	1	2	–
(15) Rogaland	100	20	2	16	2	1	26	7	–	17	5	3	–	–	7	1	–	5	4	–	–	–	6	5	–
(16) Middle Norway	–	3	–	1	1	–	3	13	–	–	–	–	–	–	–	5	–	–	1	–	–	–	1	2	–
(17) Trøndelag	26	5	–	15	1	1	32	22	4	2	2	1	2	–	1	1	–	1	2	–	–	–	1	–	–
(18) North Norway	3	1	–	2	–	–	2	–	–	–	–	–	–	–	–	–	–	–	–	1	–	–	–	–	–
(19ac) S. Finland – Onega D.	–	–	–	–	–	–	–	–	–	–	–	–	–	–	–	–	1	–	–	–	–	–	–	–	–
(19d) White Sea District	–	–	–	–	–	–	–	–	–	–	–	–	–	–	–	–	–	–	–	–	–	–	–	1	–
(19) Finland-Karelia	–	–	–	–	–	–	–	–	–	–	–	–	–	–	–	–	–	–	–	–	–	–	–	–	1
Total	535	248	27	109	68	16	242	131	19	47	23	12	6	1	38	17	3	32	29	6	5	1	124	40	1

Table 1 B–E. Ship designs by type and area.

Area	A	BIaI	bI	cI	BIIaI	bI	cI	BIIIaI	bI	cI	CIaI	bI	cI	CIIaI	bI	cI	CIIIaI	bI	cI	D	E	Total
(2a) West Denmark	3	7	2	–	–	–	–	10	1	–	1	–	–	1	–	–	–	–	–	–	1	26
(2b) Bornholm	33	1	–	2	–	–	3	1	–	4	–	–	–	–	–	–	–	–	–	2	–	46
(2) Denmark	36	8	2	2	–	–	3	11	1	4	1	–	–	1	–	–	–	–	–	2	1	72
(3) Scania	59	5	2	5	1	6	1	4	1	1	23	–	–	–	–	–	–	–	–	1	3	112
(4) South-East Sweden	39	–	3	–	5	–	3	7	2	–	–	–	–	5	–	–	–	–	–	–	2	66
(5) Östergötland	358	12	–	–	9	–	3	20	–	3	102	5	74	24	2	14	4	2	2	5	9	645
(6) Mälar District	96	3	–	–	2	5	1	16	4	–	–	–	–	4	–	–	–	–	–	5	–	136
(9) Ångermanland	187	–	–	1	4	–	–	16	–	–	–	–	2	–	–	–	–	–	–	1	9	220
(11) West Sweden	13	6	1	1	3	–	–	–	–	13	–	1	–	–	–	–	–	–	–	–	9	47
(12) Bohuslän	406	145	32	21	90	25	22	86	13	13	147	66	50	13	5	1	2	5	7	4	2	1155
(13) Østfold	122	19	5	5	28	4	9	70	3	23	18	–	4	5	–	–	–	–	–	1	–	316
(14) South Norway	74	2	–	–	7	–	3	20	4	4	–	–	1	–	–	–	–	–	–	–	–	115
(15) Rogaland	229	23	–	5	35	4	21	112	4	15	1	–	–	1	–	–	–	–	–	22	27	499
(16) Middle Norway	32	–	–	–	3	–	1	2	–	–	–	–	6	–	–	1	–	–	–	–	5	50
(17) Trøndelag	117	12	–	16	5	–	7	28	–	30	11	6	14	3	–	–	–	–	–	36	3	288
(18) North Norway	10	–	–	–	2	–	1	2	–	1	–	–	–	–	–	–	–	–	–	4	1	21
(19ac) S. Finland – Onega D.	–	–	–	–	4	–	1	16	4	–	1	–	1	–	–	–	–	–	–	–	–	27
(19d) White Sea District	2	–	–	–	–	–	–	–	–	–	17	16	13	16	–	16	5	5	5	–	13	108
(19) Finland-Karelia	2	–	–	–	4	–	1	16	4	–	18	16	14	16	–	16	5	5	5	–	13	135
Total	1780	235	45	56	198	44	72	410	33	93	344	94	171	62	36	25	11	6	15	81	66	3877

Table 2. Type-defining elements of the ship designs.

Area	Total	Horizontals					Prows			Crew			Ribs			
		A	B	C	D	E	I	II	III	a	b	c	ADE 1	BC 1	2	3
(2a) West Denmark	26	3	20	2	–	1	14	–	12	22	3	1	3	22	–	1
(2b) Bornholm	46	33	11	–	2	–	38	3	5	4	3	39	6	11	29	–
(2) Denmark	72	36	31	2	2	1	52	3	17	26	6	40	9	33	29	1
(3) Scania	112	59	19	31	–	3	101	6	5	78	6	28	62	48	1	1
(4) South-East Sweden	66	39	23	1	1	2	44	11	11	47	17	2	33	21	12	–
(5) Östergötland	645	358	44	229	5	9	505	95	45	382	35	228	240	272	102	31
(6) Mälar District	136	96	5	30	5	–	122	11	3	107	2	27	80	35	12	9
(9) Ångermanland	220	187	30	3	–	–	2	14	204	66	18	136	128	33	57	2
(11) West Sweden	47	13	27	4	1	2	23	7	17	29	9	9	11	31	3	2
(12) Bohuslän	1155	406	447	289	4	9	837	189	129	688	235	232	214	736	193	12
(13) Østfold	316	122	166	25	1	2	164	55	97	237	30	49	79	191	44	2
(14) South Norway	115	74	37	1	–	3	71	14	30	73	10	32	62	38	14	1
(15) Rogaland	499	229	219	2	22	27	230	109	160	242	32	125	218	221	56	4
(16) Middle Norway	50	32	7	6	–	5	29	14	7	11	2	37	5	13	32	–
(17) Trøndelag	288	117	98	34	36	3	167	21	100	95	29	164	95	132	46	15
(18) North Norway	21	10	7	–	4	–	8	2	11	8	7	6	12	7	2	–
(19ac) S. Finland – Onega D.	27	–	26	1	–	–	–	6	21	21	4	2	–	27	–	–
(19d) White Sea District	108	2	–	106	–	–	46	51	11	32	53	23	–	106	1	1
(19) Finland-Karelia	135	2	26	107	–	–	46	57	32	53	57	25	–	133	1	1
Total	3877	1780	1186	764	81	66	2402	608	867	2242	495	1140	1248	1944	604	81

Table 3. Type-defining elements of the ship designs. Percentages.

Area	Horizontals						Prows				Crew				Ribs				
	A	B	C	D	E		I	II	III		a	b	c		ADE 1	BC 1	2	3	
(2a) West Denmark	11.5	77	7.5	–	4	100	54	–	46	100	84.5	11.5	4	100	11.5	84.5	–	4	100
(2b) Bornholm	71.5	24	–	4.5	–	100	82.5	6.5	11	100	8.5	6.5	85	100	13	24	63	–	100
(2) Denmark	50	43.5	2.5	2.5	1.5	100	72	4	24	100	36	8.5	55.5	100	12.5	46	40	1.5	100
(3) Scania	52.5	17	27.5	–	3	100	90	5.5	4.5	100	69.5	5.5	25	100	55	43	1	1	100
(4) South-East Sweden	59	35	1.5	1.5	3	100	67	16.5	16.5	100	71	26	3	100	50	32	18	–	100
(5) Östergötland	55.5	6.5	35.5	1	1.5	100	78.5	14.5	7	100	59	5.5	35.5	100	37	42	16	5	100
(6) Mälar District	70.5	4	22	3.5	–	100	90	8	2	100	78.5	1.5	20	100	59	25.5	9	6.5	100
(9) Ångermanland	85	13.5	1.5	–	–	100	1	6	93	100	30	8	62	100	58	15	26	1	100
(11) West Sweden	27.5	57.5	8.5	2	4.5	100	49	15	36	100	62	19	19	100	23.5	66	6.5	4	100
(12) Bohuslän	35	38.5	25	0.5	1	100	72.5	16.5	11	100	59.5	20.5	20	100	18.5	64	16.5	1	100
(13) Østfold	38.5	52.5	8	0.5	0.5	100	52	17.5	30.5	100	75	9.5	15.5	100	25	60.5	14	0.5	100
(14) South Norway	64.5	32	1	–	2.5	100	62	12	26	100	63.5	8.5	28	100	54	33	12	1	100
(15) Rogaland	46	44	0.5	4	5.5	100	46	22	32	100	68.5	6.5	25	100	43.5	44.5	11	1	100
(16) Middle Norway	64	14	12	–	10	100	58	28	14	100	22	4	74	100	10	26	64	–	100
(17) Trøndelag	40.5	34	12	12.5	1	100	58	7.5	34.5	100	33	10	57	100	33	46	16	5	100
(18) North Norway	47.5	33.5	–	19	–	100	38	9.5	52.5	100	38	33.5	28.5	100	57	33.5	9.5	–	100
(19ac) S. Finland – Onega D.	–	96.5	3.5	–	–	100	–	22.5	77.5	100	77.5	15	7.5	100	–	100	–	–	100
(19d) White Sea District	2	–	98	–	–	100	42.5	47.5	10	100	29.5	49	21.5	100	–	98	1	1	100
(19) Finland-Karelia	1.5	19.5	79	–	–	100	34	42.5	23.5	100	39.5	42	18.5	100	–	99	0.5	0.5	100
Total	46	30.5	20	2	1.5	100	62	15.5	22.5	100	58	12.5	29.5	100	32.5	50	15.5	2	100

Table 4. Type defining elements of the ship designs. Control corpus.

Area	Total	Horizontals					Prows			Crew			Ribs			
		A	B	C	D	E	I	II	III	a	b	c	ADE BC	1	2	3
(3) Scania	107	54	17	33	–	3	98	2	7	80	10	17	56	50	1	–
(4) South-East Sweden	211	121	80	10	–	–	129	32	50	149	28	34	72	90	48	1
(5) Östergötland	743	456	32	248	–	7	621	94	28	439	60	244	291	280	140	32
(6) Uppland	159	105	–	49	5	–	159	–	–	125	4	30	102	49	7	1
(11) Halland–Västergötland	38	15	21	–	2	–	20	6	12	22	4	12	6	21	10	1
(12) Svenneby–Botna	539	248	236	48	3	4	419	73	47	371	44	124	197	284	55	3
(16) Hordaland	107	51	48	–	8	–	45	16	46	77	7	23	50	48	9	–

Table 5. Type-defining elements of the ship designs. Control corpus. Percentages.

Area	Horizontals						Prows				Crew				Ribs				
	A	B	C	D	E		I	II	III		a	b	c		ADE BC	1	2	3	
(3) Scania	50.5	16	31	–	2.5	100	91.5	2	6.5	100	74.5	9.5	16	100	52.5	46.5	1	–	100
(4) South-East Sweden	57.5	38	4.5	–	–	100	61	15	24	100	70.5	13.5	16	100	34	42.5	23	0.5	100
(5) Östergötland	61.5	4.5	33	–	1	100	83.5	12.5	4	100	59	8	33	100	39	37.5	19	4.5	100
(6) Uppland	66	–	31	3	–	100	100	–	–	100	78.5	2.5	19	100	64	31	4.5	0.5	100
(11) Halland–Västergötland	39.5	55.5	–	5	–	100	52.5	16	31.5	100	58	10.5	31.5	100	16	55.5	26	2.5	100
(12) Svenneby–Botna	46	44	9	0.5	0.5	100	78	13.5	8.5	100	69	8	23	100	36.5	52.5	10.5	0.5	100
(16) Hordaland	47.5	44	–	7.5	–	100	42	15	43	100	72	6.5	21.5	100	46.5	45	8.5	–	100

Table 6. Ship designs at Nämforsen, Ångermanland.

Area	AIa1	AIa2	AIc2	AIIa1	AIIa2	AIIIa1	AIIIa2	AIIIb1	AIIIb2	AIIIb3	AIIIc1	AIIIc2	AIIIc3	BIIa1	BIIb1	BIc1	BIIIa1	BIIIb1	CIIIa1	CIIIc1	Total
I, River banks	–	–	–	–	–	5	–	–	3	–	31	–	6	2	5	1	4	8	–	–	65
II, Notön	1	1	1	1	–	14	19	1	–	1	68	1	21	–	–	–	–	7	1	2	139
III, Brådön	–	–	–	–	3	1	–	3	1	–	3	–	2	2	–	–	–	1	–	–	16
Total	1	1	1	1	3	20	19	4	4	1	102	1	29	4	5	1	4	16	1	2	220

Table 7. Cart designs.

Area	A1a	A3c	B1a	B1b	B1c	B1d	B2a	B2c	B3a	C1a	C1b	C1c	C2a	C2b	C2c	C2d	Carts: total	Ships: total	%
(2) Denmark	–	–	–	–	–	–	–	–	–	–	–	–	–	–	–	–	–	72	–
(3) Scania	2	–	7	–	7	–	–	–	–	–	–	–	–	–	–	–	16	112	14.5
(4) South-East Sweden	–	–	1	–	–	–	–	–	–	–	–	–	–	–	–	–	1	66	1.5
(5) Östergötland	2	–	–	–	–	–	–	–	–	–	–	–	–	–	–	–	2	645	0.5
(6) Mälar District	–	–	–	–	–	–	–	–	–	–	–	–	–	–	–	–	–	136	–
(9) Ångermanland	–	–	–	–	–	–	–	–	–	–	–	–	–	–	–	–	–	220	–
(11) West Sweden	–	–	–	–	–	–	–	–	1	–	–	–	–	–	–	–	1	47	2
(12) Bohuslän	–	1	4	2	2	1	3	1	–	5	1	4	1	1	2	–	28	1155	2.5
(13) Østfold	–	–	1	–	–	1	–	–	–	3	–	3	–	1	–	4	13	316	4
Rest of Norway	–	–	–	–	–	–	–	–	–	–	–	–	–	–	–	–	–	973	–
(19) Finland-Karelia	–	–	–	–	–	–	–	–	–	–	–	–	–	–	–	–	–	135	–
Total	4	1	13	2	9	2	3	1	1	8	1	7	1	2	2	4	61	3877	1.5

ıble 8. Weapon designs.

Area	Axes			Daggers, swords	Spears		Ceremonial and elk-headed weapons				Weapons, total	Ships, total	%
	A1	A2	A3		S2	S3	C2	C3	E2	E3			
2) Denmark	–	–	–	–	–	–	–	–	–	–	–	72	–
3) Scania	2	78	6	–	–	–	–	–	–	–	86	112	77
4) South-East Sweden	–	4	–	–	–	–	–	–	–	–	4	66	6
5) Östergötland	–	77	–	39	6	23	–	–	–	–	145	645	22.5
6) Mälar District	–	8	–	–	9	1	–	–	–	–	18	136	13
9) Ångermanland	–	–	–	–	–	–	44	–	8	4	56	220	25.5
1) West Sweden	–	–	–	–	–	–	–	–	–	–	–	47	–
2) Bohuslän	–	–	–	–	–	9	–	–	–	–	9	1155	1
3) Østfold	–	5	–	–	–	–	–	–	–	–	5	316	1.5
5) Rogaland	–	7	–	–	–	–	–	–	–	–	7	499	1.5
6) Middle Norway	–	12	–	–	–	–	59	–	56	–	127	50	254
Rest of Norway	–	–	–	–	–	–	–	–	–	–	–	424	–
9) Finland-Karelia	–	–	–	–	–	–	–	–	–	–	–	135	–
Total	2	191	6	39	15	33	103	–	64	4	457	3877	12

Table 9. Clothing designs.

Area	Cloaks		Tunics	Clothing: total	Ships: total
	Kidney-shaped	Segment of circle			
(2) Denmark	–	–	–	–	72
(3) Scania	1	–	–	1	112
(4) South-East Sweden	–	–	–	–	66
(5) Östergötland	1	–	–	1	645
(6) Mälar District	1	2	2	5	136
(9) Ångermanland	–	–	–	–	220
(11) West Sweden	–	–	–	–	47
(12) Bohuslän	3	–	–	3	1155
Norway	–	–	–	–	1289
(19) Finland-Karelia	–	–	–	–	135
Total	6	2	2	10	3877

Table 10. Hand designs.

Area	Hand and forearm	Hand only	Hands: total	Ships: total
(1) North Germany	–	4	4	–
(2a) West Denmark	19	–	19	26
(2b) Bornholm	–	–	–	46
(2) Denmark	19	–	19	72
(12) Bohuslän	–	1	1	1155
Rest of Sweden	–	–	–	1266
(13) Østfold	2	1	3	316
(14) South Norway	–	–	–	115
(15) Rogaland	–	2	2	499
(16) Middle Norway	–	1	1	50
(17) Trøndelag	–	3	3	288
(18) North Norway	–	–	–	21
(19) Finland-Karelia	–	–	–	135
Total	21	12	33	3877

Table 11. Single foot and foot pair designs by type and area.

Area	AIa1	AIIa1	AIa2	AIIa2	AIb2	AIIb2	BIa1	BIIa1	BIa2	BIIa2	BIb1	BIIb1	BIb2	BIIb2	Foot designs, total
(2a) West Denmark	–	2	–	–	–	–	13	4	–	–	–	–	–	–	19
(2b) Bornholm	2	–	–	–	–	–	12	2	–	–	–	–	–	–	16
(2) Denmark	2	2	–	–	–	–	25	6	–	–	–	–	–	–	35
(3) Scania	58	10	–	–	–	–	15	7	–	1	–	–	16	13	120
(4) South-East Sweden	–	1	2	–	–	–	2	1	–	–	1	–	1	9	17
(5) Östergötland	–	–	–	–	–	–	9	3	53	32	–	2	10	17	126
(6) Mälar District	–	–	–	–	–	–	7	–	1	1	–	–	2	1	12
(9) Ångermanland	–	–	–	–	–	–	–	–	5	2	–	–	3	8	18
(11) West Sweden	–	–	–	–	–	–	52	35	5	6	5	6	–	1	110
(12) Bohuslän	7	8	2	1	2	–	10	21	6	3	–	–	20	11	91
(13) Østfold	2	–	–	–	–	–	2	2	1	–	–	–	6	1	14
(14) South Norway	–	–	2	–	1	–	6	–	–	4	–	–	7	9	29
(15) Rogaland	–	–	–	4	–	1	7	5	48	12	–	–	7	3	87
(16) Middle Norway	–	–	–	–	–	–	–	3	–	–	–	–	–	–	3
(17) Trøndelag	–	–	–	–	–	–	23	–	–	10	–	–	11	11	55
(18) North Norway	–	–	–	–	–	–	–	–	–	–	–	–	–	5	5
(19d) White Sea District	14	–	2	–	–	–	–	–	–	–	–	–	–	–	16
(19) Finland-Karelia	14	–	2	–	–	–	–	–	–	–	–	–	–	–	16
Total	83	21	8	5	3	1	158	83	119	71	6	8	83	89	738
Single feet, total	125		18		5		324		261		22		261		1016

Table 12. Type-defining elements of the single foot designs.

Area	Foot/shoe		Single/pair				Feet, total	Ships, total	%
	A	B	AI	AII	BI	BII			
(2a) West Denmark	4	21	–	4	13	8	25	26	96
(2b) Bornholm	2	16	2	–	12	4	18	46	39
(2) Denmark	6	37	2	4	25	12	43	72	59.5
(3) Scania	78	73	58	20	31	42	151	112	135
(4) South-East Sweden	4	24	2	2	4	20	28	66	42.5
(5) Östergötland	–	150	–	–	78	108	180	645	28
(6) Mälar District	–	14	–	–	10	4	14	136	10
(9) Ångermanland	–	28	–	–	8	20	28	220	12.5
(11) West Sweden	–	158	–	–	62	96	158	47	336
(12) Bohuslän	29	106	11	18	36	70	135	1155	11.5
(13) Østfold	2	15	2	–	9	6	17	316	5.5
(14) South Norway	3	39	3	–	13	26	42	115	36.5
(15) Rogaland	10	102	–	10	62	40	112	499	22.5
(16) Middle Norway	–	6	–	–	–	6	6	50	12
(17) Trøndelag	–	76	–	–	34	42	76	288	26.5
(18) North Norway	–	10	–	–	–	10	10	21	47.5
(19) Finland-Karelia	16	–	16	–	–	–	16	135	12
Total	148	868	94	54	366	502	1016	3877	26

Table 13. Type-defining elements of the single foot designs. Percentages.

Area	Foot/shoe		Single/pair				Total
	A	B	AI	AII	BI	BII	
(2a) West Denmark	16	84	–	100	62	38	25
(2b) Bornholm	11	89	100	–	75	25	18
(2) Denmark	14	86	33.5	66.5	67.5	32.5	43
(3) Scania	51.5	48.5	74.5	25.5	42.5	57.5	151
(4) South-East Sweden	14.5	85.5	50	50	16.5	83.5	28
(5) Östergötland	–	100	–	–	40	60	180
(6) Mälar District	–	100	–	–	71.5	28.5	14
(9) Ångermanland	–	100	–	–	28.5	71.5	28
(11) West Sweden	–	100	–	–	39	61	158
(12) Bohuslän	21.5	78.5	38	62	34	66	135
(13) Østfold	12	88	100	–	60	40	17
(14) South Norway	7	93	100	–	33.5	66.5	42
(15) Rogaland	9	91	–	100	61	39	112
(16) Middle Norway	–	100	–	–	–	100	6
(17) Trøndelag	–	100	–	–	44.5	55.5	76
(18) North Norway	–	100	–	–	–	100	10
(19) Finland-Karelia	100	–	100	–	–	–	16
Total	14.5	85.5	63.5	36.5	42	58	1016

Table 14. Type-defining elements of the single foot designs. Control corpus.

Area	Foot/ shoe		Single/pair				Feet, total	Ships, total	%
	A	B	AI	AII	BI	BII			
(1) North Germany	3	2	3	–	2	–	5	–	–
(3) Scania	112	92	91	21	36	56	204	107	*190.5*
(4) South-East Sweden	2	53	2	–	13	40	55	211	*26*
(5) Östergötland	9	143	7	2	48	95	152	743	*20.5*
(6) Uppland	1	69	1	–	6	63	70	159	*44*
(11) Halland–Västergötland	9	118	9	–	34	84	127	38	*334*
(12) Svenneby-Bottna	3	30	3	–	18	12	33	539	*6*
(16) Hordaland	2	60	2	–	20	40	62	107	*58*

Table 15. Type-defining elements of the single foot designs. Control corpus. Percentages.

Area	Foot/ shoe		Single/pair				Total
	A	B	AI	AII	BI	BII	
(1) North Germany	60	40	100	–	100	–	5
(3) Scania	55	45	81.5	18.5	39	61	204
(4) South-East Sweden	3.5	96.5	100	–	24.5	75.5	55
(5) Östergötland	6	94	78	22	33.5	66.5	152
(6) Uppland	1.5	98.5	100	–	8.5	91.5	70
(11) Halland-Västergötland	7	93	100	–	29	71	127
(12) Svenneby-Bottna	9	91	100	–	60	40	33
(16) Hordaland	3	97	100	–	33.5	66.5	62

Table 16. Foot designs at Nämforsen, Ångermanland.

Area	BIa2	BIIa2	BIb2	BIIb2	Foot designs, total
I, River banks	1	–	–	1	2
II, Notön	1	1	–	–	2
III, Brådön	3	1	3	7	14
Single feet, total	5	4	3	16	28

Table 17. Circle designs by type and area.

Area	Unconnected										With ship		With stand		Circles, total	Ships, total	%
	A0a	A0b	A1a	A1b	B0a	B0b	B1a	C0a	C0b	18 other types	A0a1	6 other types	A4aII	7 other types			
(2a) West Denmark	18	6	78	3	3	–	–	4	–	6	1	–	–	–	119	26	457.5
(2b) Bornholm	1	2	13	1	–	–	1	–	–	–	–	1	–	–	19	46	41.5
(2) Denmark	19	8	91	4	3	–	1	4	–	6	1	1	–	–	138	72	191.5
(3) Scania	12	–	35	–	–	–	5	–	–	–	–	–	–	–	52	112	46.5
(4) South-East Sweden	–	–	9	–	1	–	1	5	1	4	–	–	–	–	21	66	32
(5) Östergötland	8	2	39	2	1	1	2	2	3	7	1	1	–	2	71	645	11
(6) Mälar District	1	3	1	–	–	–	–	–	1	4	–	–	–	–	10	136	7.5
(9) Ångermanland	–	–	2	–	–	–	–	–	–	–	–	–	–	–	2	220	1
(11) West Sweden	3	2	14	2	–	2	1	–	1	6	–	–	–	–	26	47	55.5
(12) Bohuslän	17	8	33	2	1	2	2	–	2	10	3	11	2	10	100	1155	8.5
(13) Østfold	15	2	12	–	1	2	2	1	2	7	3	–	–	–	47	316	15
(14) South Norway	4	–	2	–	–	–	–	–	1	11	–	–	–	–	18	115	15.5
(15) Rogaland	13	2	5	3	13	7	–	8	3	1	1	–	–	4	60	499	12
(16) Middle Norway	10	1	4	1	2	–	1	9	2	3	–	–	–	–	33	50	66
(17) Trøndelag	10	10	3	–	4	4	–	2	1	2	1	–	–	1	38	288	13
(18) North Norway	–	–	1	–	–	–	–	–	–	–	–	–	–	–	1	21	5
(19ac) S. Finland – Onega D.	–	–	–	–	–	–	–	–	–	–	–	1	29	1	31	27	115
(19) Finland-Karelia	–	–	–	–	–	–	–	–	–	–	–	1	29	1	31	135	23
Total	112	38	251	12	26	16	13	31	15	61	10	14	31	18	648	3877	16.5

Table 18. Type-defining elements of the circle designs.

Area	Total	Concentric circles			Radii						Additions			Connections		
		A	B	C	0	1	11	2	3	4	a	b	c	No	I	II
(2a) West Denmark	119	112	3	4	33	81	–	4	1	–	107	10	2	118	1	–
(2b) Bornholm	19	18	1	–	3	16	–	–	–	–	16	3	–	18	1	–
(2) Denmark	138	130	4	4	36	97	–	4	1	–	123	13	2	136	2	–
(3) Scania	52	47	5	–	12	40	–	–	–	–	52	–	–	52	–	–
(4) South-East Sweden	21	12	2	7	9	11	–	–	1	–	17	1	3	21	2	–
(5) Östergötland	71	58	5	8	21	44	–	3	3	–	59	11	1	67	2	2
(6) Mälar District	10	6	4	–	5	1	–	–	4	–	6	4	–	10	–	–
(9) Ångermanland	2	2	–	–	–	2	–	–	–	–	2	–	–	2	–	–
(11) West Sweden	26	25	–	1	6	14	–	6	–	–	22	4	–	26	–	–
(12) Bohuslän	100	85	14	1	42	45	–	6	3	4	81	16	3	74	14	12
(13) Østfold	47	35	8	4	27	16	–	1	3	–	37	9	1	44	3	–
(14) South Norway	18	14	2	2	5	2	11	–	–	–	7	11	–	18	1	–
(15) Rogaland	60	25	21	14	50	9	–	–	1	–	42	18	–	55	1	4
(16) Middle Norway	33	19	3	11	24	6	–	–	3	–	26	7	–	33	–	–
(17) Trøndelag	38	26	8	4	33	5	–	–	–	–	22	15	1	36	1	1
(18) North Norway	1	1	–	–	–	–	–	–	–	1	1	–	–	1	–	–
(19ac) S. Finland – Onega D.	31	31	–	–	1	1	–	–	–	29	31	–	–	–	1	30
(19) Finland-Karelia	31	31	–	–	1	1	–	–	–	29	31	–	–	–	1	30
Total	648	516	76	56	271	294	11	20	19	33	528	108	11	575	24	49

Table 19. Type-defining elements of the circle designs. Percentages.

Area	Concentric circles				Radii							Additions				Connections			
	A	B	C		0	1	11	2	3	4		a	b	c		No	I	II	
(2a) West Denmark	94	2.5	3.5	100	27.5	68	–	3.5	1	–	100	90	8.5	1.5	100	99	1	–	100
(2b) Bornholm	94.5	5.5	–	100	16	84	–	3	–	–	100	84	16	–	100	94.5	5.5	–	100
(2) Denmark	94	3	3	100	26	70	–	3	1	–	100	89	9.5	1.5	100	98.5	1.5	–	100
(3) Scania	90.5	9.5	–	100	23	77	–	–	–	–	100	100	–	–	100	100	–	–	100
(4) South East Sweden	57	9.5	33.5	100	43	52.5	–	–	4.5	–	100	81	5	14	100	100	–	–	100
(5) Östergötland	81.5	7	11.5	100	29.5	62	–	4.5	4	–	100	83	15.5	1.5	100	94	3	3	100
(6) Mälar District	60	40	–	100	50	10	–	–	40	–	100	60	40	–	100	100	–	–	100
(9) Ångermanland	100	–	–	100	–	100	–	–	–	–	100	100	–	–	100	100	–	–	100
(11) West Sweden	96	–	4	100	23	54	–	23	–	–	100	84.5	15.5	–	100	100	–	–	100
(12) Bohuslän	85	14	1	100	42	45	–	6	3	4	100	81	16	3	100	74	14	12	100
(13) Østfold	74.5	17	8.5	100	57.5	34	–	2	6.5	–	100	79	19	2	100	93.5	6.5	–	100
(14) South Norway	78	11	11	100	28	11	61	–	–	–	100	39	61	–	100	100	–	–	100
(15) Rogaland	41.5	35	23.5	100	83.5	15	–	–	1.5	–	100	70	30	–	100	92	1.5	6.5	100
(16) Middle Norway	57.5	9	33.5	100	73	18	–	–	9	–	100	79	21	–	100	100	–	–	100
(17) Trøndelag	68.5	21	10.5	100	87	13	–	–	–	–	100	58	39.5	2.5	100	95	2.5	2.5	100
(18) North Norway	100	–	–	100	–	100	–	–	–	–	100	100	–	–	100	100	–	–	100
(19ac) S. Finland – Onega D.	100	–	–	100	3.5	3	–	–	–	93.5	100	100	–	–	100	–	3	97	100
(19) Finland-Karelia	100	–	–	100	3.5	3	–	–	–	93.5	100	100	–	–	100	–	3	97	100
Total	79.5	12	8.5	100	42	45.5	1.5	3	3	5	100	81.5	16.5	2	100	88.5	4	7.5	100

Table 20. Type-defining elements of the circle designs. Control corpus.

Area	Concentric circles			Radii						Additions			Connections			Circles, total	Ships, total	%
	A	B	C	0	1	11	2	3	4	a	b	c	No	I	II			
(1) North Germany	6	3	–	5	2	–	1	1	–	5	4	–	9	–	–	9	–	–
(3) Scania	64	3	–	8	59	–	–	–	–	66	1	–	67	–	–	67	107	62.5
(4) South-East Sweden	9	2	3	9	5	1	–	–	–	9	5	–	14	3	–	14	211	6.5
(5) Östergötland	48	2	21	28	32	1	5	5	–	53	18	–	68	–	–	71	743	9.5
(6) Uppland	12	2	9	11	12	–	–	–	–	16	5	2	23	–	–	*23*	*159*	*14.5*
(11) Halland-Västergötland	33	1	–	3	21	–	5	5	–	32	1	1	34	–	–	*34*	*38*	*89.5*
(12) Svenneby-Bottna	41	2	1	23	20	–	–	1	–	33	10	1	37	2	5	44	539	8
(16) Hordaland	32	9	33	47	18	–	–	9	–	27	40	7	74	–	–	74	107	69

Table 21. Type-defining elements of the circle designs. Control corpus. Percentages.

Area	Concentric circles			Radii						Additions			Connections		
	A	B	C	0	1	11	2	3	4	a	b	c	No	I	II
(1) North Germany	67	33	–	55.5	22.5	–	11	11	–	55.5	43.5	–	100	–	–
(3) Scania	96	4	–	12	88	–	–	–	–	98.5	1.5	–	100	–	–
(4) South-East Sweden	64	14.5	21.5	64.5	35.5	–	–	–	–	64.5	35.5	–	100	–	–
(5) Östergötland	67.5	3	29.5	39.5	45	1.5	7	7	–	74.5	25.5	–	96	4	–
(6) Uppland	52	9	39	48	52	–	–	–	–	69.5	21.5	9	100	–	–
(11) Halland-Västergötland	97	3	–	9	62	–	14.5	14.5	–	94	3	3	100	–	–
(12) Svenneby-Bottna	93	4.5	2.5	52.5	45.5	–	–	2	–	75	22.5	2.5	84	4.5	11.5
(16) Hordaland	43.5	12	44.5	63.5	24.5	–	–	12	–	36.5	54.	9.5	100	–	–

Table 22. Human figures by type and area.

Area	AIa0	AIa+	AIb0	AIIa0	AIIa+	BIa0	BIa+	CIa0	CIa+	CIIa+	CIIa++	36 other types	Human figures, total	Ships, total	%
(1) North Germany	1	1	–	–	–	–	–	–	–	–	–	–	3	–	–
(2a) West Denmark	4	–	1	–	1	–	–	–	–	–	–	4	10	26	38.5
(2b) Bornholm	–	–	–	–	–	–	–	–	–	–	–	1	1	46	2
(2) Denmark	4	–	1	–	1	–	–	–	–	–	–	5	11	72	15
(3) Scania	1	10	–	–	–	6	8	–	–	–	–	17	42	112	37.5
(4) South-East Sweden	–	–	–	–	–	–	–	–	–	–	–	–	–	66	–
(5) Östergötland	42	13	–	–	1	11	20	–	–	–	–	13	100	645	15.5
(6) Mälar District	1	2	1	–	–	32	23	–	–	–	–	5	64	136	47
(8) Jämtland	11	–	–	–	–	–	–	–	–	–	–	1	12	–	–
(9) Ångermanland	51	–	–	2	–	–	–	–	–	–	–	–	53	220	24
(11) West Sweden	2	–	1	–	1	–	–	1	2	–	–	5	12	47	25.5
(12) Bohuslän	47	25	12	29	26	22	20	11	10	21	23	176	422	1155	36.5
(13) Østfold	20	2	4	1	–	–	5	1	3	–	–	16	51	316	16
(14) South Norway	8	1	2	–	1	4	4	–	–	–	–	–	16	115	14
(15) Rogaland	2	–	–	–	–	–	–	–	–	–	–	1	8	499	1.5
(16) Middle Norway	8	–	2	–	–	3	2	–	–	–	–	–	10	50	20
(17) Trøndelag	36	5	2	6	2	–	–	–	–	–	–	19	75	288	26
(18) North Norway	11	–	–	–	–	–	2	2	–	–	–	1	14	21	66.5
(19ac) S. Finland – Onega D.	30	4	3	1	–	–	–	3	4	1	–	7	53	27	196.5
(19d) White Sea District	13	15	2	2	9	–	–	3	4	19	2	19	88	108	81.5
(19) Finland-Karelia	43	19	5	3	9	–	–	6	8	20	2	26	141	135	104.5
Total	288	78	31	41	41	78	82	21	23	41	25	285	1034	3877	26.5

Table 23. Type-defining elements of the human figures.

Area	Total	Legs					Position			Fingers		Number of attributes				Attributes							
		A	B	C	D	E	I	II	III	a	b	0	+	++	+++	0	1	2	3	4	5	6	7
(1) North Germany	3	3	–	–	–	–	3	–	–	3	–	2	1	–	–	2	–	1	–	–	–	–	–
(2a) West Denmark	10	10	–	–	–	–	6	3	1	6	4	8	2	–	–	8	1	–	1	–	–	–	–
(2b) Bornholm	1	–	–	1	–	–	–	1	–	–	1	1	–	–	–	1	–	–	–	–	–	–	–
(2) Denmark	11	10	–	1	–	–	6	4	1	6	5	9	2	–	–	9	1	–	1	–	–	–	–
(3) Scania	42	11	14	1	–	16	41	1	–	41	1	23	19	–	–	23	5	–	–	–	–	8	6
(4) South-East Sweden	–	–	–	–	–	–	–	–	–	–	–	–	–	–	–	–	–	–	–	–	–	–	–
(5) Östergötland	100	60	36	1	3	–	92	6	2	98	2	58	40	3	–	57	34	–	7	–	2	3	–
(6) Mälar District	64	4	55	–	5	–	64	–	–	63	1	37	26	1	–	37	5	–	–	–	22	1	–
(8) Jämtland	12	11	–	–	–	1	12	–	–	12	–	12	–	–	–	12	–	–	–	–	–	–	–
(9) Ångermanland	53	53	–	–	–	–	51	2	–	53	–	53	–	–	–	53	–	–	–	–	–	–	–
(11) West Sweden	12	4	–	5	1	2	9	3	–	9	3	9	3	–	–	9	1	–	2	–	–	–	–
(12) Bohuslän	422	183	80	101	33	25	213	182	27	383	39	173	163	67	19	173	168	39	33	9	41	37	27
(13) Østfold	51	30	5	5	11	–	43	8	–	47	4	30	17	1	3	30	14	1	1	2	8	–	2
(14) South Norway	16	12	4	–	–	–	15	1	–	14	2	11	5	–	–	11	1	–	1	–	4	–	–
(15) Rogaland	8	3	5	–	–	–	6	2	–	8	–	7	1	–	–	7	1	–	–	–	–	–	–
(16) Middle Norway	10	10	–	–	–	–	10	–	–	8	2	10	–	–	–	10	–	–	–	–	–	–	–
(17) Trøndelag	75	56	8	2	4	5	55	19	1	69	6	57	18	–	–	57	8	–	–	–	–	–	10
(18) North Norway	14	12	–	2	2	–	14	–	–	13	1	13	1	–	–	13	–	–	–	–	–	1	–
(19ac) S. Finland – Onega D.	53	39	–	11	2	1	48	5	–	48	5	43	9	1	–	43	1	–	3	–	–	7	–
(19d) White Sea District	88	47	–	41	–	–	50	38	–	81	7	22	51	14	1	22	17	–	6	13	–	46	–
(19) Finland-Karelia	141	86	–	52	2	1	98	43	–	129	12	65	60	15	1	65	18	–	9	13	–	53	–
Total	1034	548	207	170	59	50	732	271	31	955	79	568	356	87	23	568	256	41	53	24	77	103	45

Table 24. Type-defining elements of the human figures. Percentages.

Area	Legs					Position			Fingers		Number of attributes				Attributes							
	A	B	C	D	E	I	II	III	a	b	0	+	++	+++	0	1	2	3	4	5	6	7
(1) North Germany	100	–	–	–	–	100	–	–	66.5	33.5	66.5	33.5	–	–	66.5	–	33.5	–	–	–	–	–
(2a) West Denmark	100	–	–	–	–	60	30	10	60	40	80	20	–	–	80	10	–	10	–	–	–	–
(2b) Bornholm	–	–	100	–	–	–	100	–	–	100	100	–	–	–	100	–	–	–	–	–	–	–
(2) Denmark	91	–	9	–	–	54.5	36.5	9	54.5	45.5	82	18	–	–	82	9	–	9	–	–	–	–
(3) Scania	26	33.5	2.5	–	38	97.5	2.5	–	97.5	2.5	55	45	–	–	55	12	–	–	–	–	19	14
(4) South-East Sweden	–	–	–	–	–	–	–	–	–	–	–	–	–	–	–	–	–	–	–	–	–	–
(5) Östergötland	60	36	1	3	–	92	6	2	98	2	57	40	3	–	57	34	2	7	–	–	–	–
(6) Mälar District	6.5	86	–	7.5	–	100	–	–	98.5	1.5	58	40.5	1.5	–	58	8	–	–	–	34	1.5	–
(8) Jämtland	91.5	–	–	–	8.5	100	–	–	100	–	100	–	–	–	100	–	–	–	–	–	–	–
(9) Ångermanland	100	–	–	–	–	96	4	–	100	–	100	–	–	–	100	–	–	–	–	–	–	–
(11) West Sweden	33.5	–	41.5	8.5	16.5	75	25	–	75	25	75	25	–	–	75	8.5	9	16.5	–	–	–	–
(12) Bohuslän	43.5	19	24	7.5	6	50.5	43	6.5	91	9	41	38.5	16	4.5	41	40	9	8	2	9.5	9	6.5
(13) Østfold	59	10	10	21	–	84.5	15.5	–	92	8	59	33	2	6	60	27.5	2	2	4	–	–	4
(14) South Norway	75	25	–	–	–	93.5	6.5	–	87.5	12.5	69	31	–	–	69	6	–	–	–	25	–	–
(15) Rogaland	37.5	62.5	–	–	–	75	25	–	100	–	87.5	12.5	–	–	87.5	12.5	–	–	–	–	–	–
(16) Middle Norway	100	–	–	–	–	100	–	–	80	20	100	–	–	–	100	–	–	–	–	–	–	–
(17) Trøndelag	75	10.5	2.5	5.5	6.5	73.5	25.5	1	92	8	76	24	–	–	76	10.5	–	–	–	–	–	13.5
(18) North Norway	85.5	–	14.5	–	–	100	–	–	93	7	93	7	–	–	93	–	–	–	–	–	7	–
(19ac) S. Finland – Onega D.	73.5	–	20.5	4	2	90.5	9.5	–	90.5	9.5	81	17	2	–	81	2	–	5.5	–	–	13	–
(19d) White Sea District	53.5	–	46.5	–	–	57	43	–	92	8	25	58	16	1	25	19.5	–	7	15	15.5	52	–
(19) Finland-Karelia	61	–	37	1.5	0.5	69.5	30.5	–	91.5	8.5	46	42.5	10.5	1	46	13	–	6.5	9	–	37.5	–
Total	53	20	16.5	5.5	5	70.5	26.5	3	92.5	7.5	55	34.5	8.5	2	55	25	4	5	2.5	7.5	10	4.5

Table 25 a. Animal designs by type and area. South region.

Area	A2	A4	B2	B4	C2	C4	D2	D4	AF0	AF2	BF0	BF2	CF0	CF2	DF0	DF2	AO	DO	AV	BV	CV	Animal figures, total	Ships, total	%
(1) North Germany	–	–	–	–	–	–	–	–	–	–	–	–	–	–	–	–	–	–	–	–	–	–	–	–
(2a) West Denmark	–	–	–	–	–	–	3	3	–	–	–	–	–	–	–	–	1	–	–	–	–	7	26	27
(2b) Bornholm	–	–	–	–	–	–	–	–	–	–	–	–	–	–	–	–	–	–	–	–	–	–	46	0
(2) Denmark	–	–	–	–	–	–	3	3	–	–	–	–	–	–	–	–	1	–	–	–	–	7	72	9.5
(3) Scania	–	–	–	–	–	8	1	3	–	–	–	–	–	–	–	–	–	4	–	–	–	17	112	15
(4) South-East Sweden	–	–	–	–	1	–	5	2	–	–	–	–	–	–	–	–	–	1	–	–	–	9	66	13.5
(5) Östergötland	–	4	–	4	74	114	10	68	–	–	–	–	–	1	–	–	–	–	–	–	–	275	645	42.5
(6) Mälar District	–	–	2	–	18	19	1	1	–	–	–	–	–	–	–	–	–	–	–	–	–	41	136	30
(11) West Sweden	1	–	1	–	–	3	–	8	–	–	–	–	–	–	–	–	–	14	–	–	–	27	47	57.5
(12) Bohuslän	–	4	–	2	8	43	77	254	–	–	–	–	–	10	–	22	–	4	–	–	–	424	1155	36.5
(13) Østfold	–	–	2	2	–	–	1	16	–	–	–	–	–	–	–	–	–	–	–	–	–	21	316	6.5
(14) South Norway	4	–	8	8	1	–	–	10	–	–	–	1	–	–	–	–	–	–	–	4	–	37	115	32
(15) Rogaland	–	–	–	–	–	1	–	–	1	–	–	–	–	–	–	–	–	1	2	–	–	4	499	1
South region, total	5	8	13	16	102	188	98	365	1	–	–	1	–	11	–	22	2	24	2	4	–	862	3163	27.5

Table 25 b. Animal designs by type and area. North region.

Area	A2	A4	B2	B4	C2	C4	D2	D4	AF0	AF2	BF0	BF2	CF0	CF2	DF0	DF2	AO	DO	AV	BV	CV	Animal figures, total	Ships, total	%
(8) Jämtland	19	7	36	7	1	–	–	–	–	–	–	–	–	–	–	–	–	–	–	–	–	70	–	∞
(9) Ångermanland	174	–	48	–	217	1	11	–	–	–	–	1	–	2	–	–	–	–	6	–	5	465	220	211
(16) Middle Norway	8	8	67	172	12	20	6	9	–	–	–	–	–	–	–	–	–	–	9	1	–	292	50	584
(17) Trøndelag	24	1	12	4	–	1	133	–	7	1	1	–	–	1	–	–	–	–	1	25	–	209	288	73
(18a) Nordland	52	–	1	–	–	–	1	–	1	1	–	–	–	1	–	–	–	–	13	4	–	74	17	435
(18b) Troms-Finnmark	9	9	8	5	–	–	5	1	–	–	–	–	–	–	–	–	–	–	13	–	–	50	4	1250
(18) North Norway	61	9	9	5	–	–	6	1	1	–	–	1	–	–	–	–	–	–	26	4	–	124	21	590
(19a) South Finland	2	–	8	–	–	–	–	1	–	–	–	–	–	–	–	–	–	–	–	–	1	12	7	171
(19c) Onega District	6	–	3	–	36	3	7	–	11	7	1	10	14	43	19	6	–	1	–	–	5	172	20	860
(19d) White Sea District	–	–	–	–	96	–	5	1	–	–	–	–	–	5	3	4	–	–	–	–	60	173	108	160
(19) Finland-Karelia	8	–	11	–	132	3	12	1	11	7	1	10	14	48	22	10	–	1	–	–	66	357	135	264
North region, total	294	25	183	168	362	25	168	11	19	8	2	12	14	50	22	10	–	1	42	30	71	1517	714	212
South region, total	5	8	13	16	102	188	98	365	1	–	–	1	–	11	·	22	2	24	2	4	–	862	3163	27.5
Total	299	33	196	184	464	213	266	376	20	8	2	13	14	61	22	32	2	25	44	34	71	2379	3877	61.5

Table 26 a. Type-defining elements of the quadruped designs. South region.

Area	Total	Species										Body				Ears, horns, antlers				Legs	
		a	b	c	h	n	s	Qua-drupeds	F	O	V	A	B	C	D	I	II	X	XI	2	4
(2a) West Denmark	7	3	–	3	–	–	–	6	–	1	–	–	–	–	6	–	5	1	–	3	3
(2b) Bornholm	–	–	–	–	–	–	–	–	–	–	–	–	–	–	–	–	–	–	–	–	–
(2) Denmark	7	3	–	3	–	–	–	6	–	1	–	–	–	–	6	–	5	1	–	3	3
(3) Scania	17	7	–	–	5	–	–	12	–	5	–	–	–	8	4	6	6	–	–	1	11
(4) South-East Sweden	9	3	–	–	5	–	–	8	–	1	–	–	–	1	7	5	3	–	–	6	2
(5) Östergötland	275	197	–	12	19	2	44	274	1	–	–	4	4	188	78	158	104	12	–	84	190
(6) Mälar District	41	20	–	–	–	4	17	41	–	–	–	–	2	37	2	10	31	–	–	21	20
(11) West Sweden	27	13	–	–	25	–	–	13	–	14	–	1	1	3	8	6	7	–	–	2	11
(12) Bohuslän	424	312	–	23	–	28	–	388	32	4	–	4	2	51	331	57	307	24	–	85	303
(13) Østfold	21	17	–	4	–	–	–	21	–	–	–	–	4	–	17	12	9	–	–	3	18
(14) South Norway	37	22	–	9	–	–	–	31	2	–	4	4	16	1	10	10	17	–	4	13	18
(15) Rogaland	4	1	–	–	–	–	–	1	–	–	2	–	–	1	–	1	–	–	–	–	1
South region, total	862	595	–	51	54	34	61	795	35	26	6	13	29	290	463	265	489	37	4	218	577

Table 26 b. Type-defining elements of the quadruped designs. North region.

Area	Total	Species										Body				Ears, horns, antlers				Legs	
		a	b	c	h	n	s	Qua-dru-peds	F	O	V	A	B	C	D	I	II	X	XI	2	4
(8) Jämtland	70	57	–	13	–	–	–	70	–	–	–	26	43	1	–	–	63	6	1	56	14
(9) Ångermanland	465	379	–	72	–	–	–	451	3	–	11	174	48	218	11	10	435	1	5	450	1
(16) Middle Norway	292	267	–	15	–	–	–	282	–	–	10	16	219	32	15	14	240	25	3	93	189
(17) Trøndelag	209	158	–	17	–	–	–	175	8	–	26	25	16	1	133	111	55	4	5	169	6
(18a) Nordland	74	6	5	43	–	–	–	54	3	–	17	52	1	–	1	1	26	23	4	54	–
(18b) Troms-Finnmark	50	32	1	4	–	–	–	37	–	–	13	18	13	–	6	1	25	8	3	22	15
(18) North Norway	124	38	6	47	–	–	–	91	3	–	30	70	14	–	7	2	51	31	7	76	15
(19a) South Finland	12	11	–	–	–	–	–	11	–	–	1	2	8	–	–	–	11	–	–	10	1
(19c) Onega District	172	25	–	30	–	–	–	55	111	1	5	6	3	39	7	5	49	1	–	52	3
(19d) White Sea District	173	57	1	43	–	–	–	101	12	–	60	–	–	96	5	–	84	15	2	101	–
(19) Finland-Karelia	357	93	1	73	–	–	–	167	123	1	66	8	11	135	13	5	144	16	2	163	4
North region, total	1517	992	7	237	–	–	–	1236	137	1	143	319	351	387	179	142	988	83	23	1007	229
South region, total	862	595	–	51	54	34	61	795	35	26	6	13	29	290	463	265	489	37	4	218	577
Total	2379	1587	7	288	54	34	61	2031	172	27	149	332	380	677	642	407	1477	120	27	1225	806

Table 27 a. Type-defining elements of the quadruped designs. South region. Percentages.

Area	Species										Body				Ears, horns, antlers				Legs	
	a	b	c	h	n	s	Quadrupeds	F	O	V	A	B	C	D	I	II	X	XI	2	4
(2a) West Denmark	43	–	43	–	–	–	86	–	14	–	–	–	–	100	–	83.5	16.5	–	50	50
(2b) Bornholm	–	–	–	–	–	–	–	–	–	–	–	–	–	–	–	–	–	–	–	–
(2) Denmark	43	–	43	–	–	–	86	–	14	–	–	–	–	100	–	83.5	1.5	–	50	50
(3) Scania	41	–	–	29.5	–	–	70.5	–	29.5	–	–	–	66.5	33.5	50	50	–	–	8.5	91.5
(4) South-East Sweden	33.5	–	55.5	–	–	–	89	–	11	–	–	–	12.5	87.5	62.5	37.5	–	–	75	25
(5) Östergötland	71.5	–	4.5	7	0.5	16	99.5	0.5	–	–	1.5	1.5	68.5	28.5	57.5	38	4.5	–	30.5	69.5
(6) Mälar District	48.5	–	–	–	10	41.5	100	–	–	–	–	5	90	5	24.5	75.5	–	–	51	49
(11) West Sweden	48	–	–	–	–	–	48	–	52	–	7.5	7.5	23.5	61.5	46	54	–	–	15.5	84.5
(12) Bohuslän	73.5	–	5.5	6	6.5	–	91.5	7.5	1	–	1	0.5	13	85.5	15	79	6	–	22	78
(13) Østfold	81	–	19	–	–	–	100	–	–	–	–	19	–	81	57	43	–	–	14.5	85.5
(14) South Norway	59.5	–	24	–	–	–	84	5.5	–	11	13	51.5	3	32.5	32	55	–	13	42	58
(15) Rogaland	25	–	–	–	–	–	25	–	25	50	–	–	100	–	100	–	–	–	–	100
South region, total	69	–	6	6.5	4	7	92.5	4	3	0.5	1.5	3.5	36.5	58.5	33.5	61.5	4.5	0.5	27.5	72.5

Table 27 b. Type-defining elements of the quadruped designs. North region. Percentages.

Area	Species										Body				Ears, horns, antlers				Legs	
	a	b	c	h	n	s	Qua-drupeds	F	O	V	A	B	C	D	I	II	X	XI	2	4
(8) Jämtland	81.5	–	18.5	–	–	–	100	–	–	–	37	61.5	1.5	–	–	90	8.5	1.5	80	20
(9) Ångermanland	81.5	–	15.5	–	–	–	97	0.5	–	2.5	38.5	10.5	48.5	2.5	2	96.5	0.5	1	99.5	0.5
(16) Middle Norway	91.5	–	5	–	–	–	96.5	–	–	3.5	5.5	77.5	11.5	5.5	5	85	9	1	33	67
(17) Trøndelag	75.5	–	8	–	–	–	83.5	4	–	12.5	14.5	9	0.5	76	63.5	31.5	2.5	2.5	96.5	3.5
(18a) Nordland	8	7	58	–	–	–	73	4	–	23	96	2	–	2	2	48	42.5	7.5	100	–
(18b) Troms-Finnmark	64	2	8	–	–	–	74	–	–	26	48.5	35	–	16.5	3	67.5	21.5	8	59.5	40.5
(18) North Norway	30.5	5	38	–	–	–	73.5	2.5	–	24	77	15.5	–	7.5	2.5	56	34	7.5	83.5	16.5
(19a) South Finland	91.5	–	–	–	–	–	91.5	–	–	8.5	18	73	–	9	–	100	–	–	91	9
(19c) Onega District	14.5	–	17.5	–	–	–	32	64.5	0.5	3	11	5.5	71	12.5	9	89	2	–	94.5	5.5
(19d) White Sea District	33	0.5	25	–	–	–	58.5	7	–	34.5	–	–	95	5	–	83	15	2	100	–
(19) Finland-Karelia	26	0.5	20.5	–	–	–	47	34.5	0.5	18	5	6.5	81	7.5	3	86.5	9.5	1	97.5	2.5
North region, total	65.5	0.5	15.5	–	–	–	81.5	9	0	9.5	26	28.5	31	14.5	11.5	80	6.5	2	81.5	18.5
South region, total	69	–	6	6.5	4	7	92.5	4	3	0.5	1.5	3.5	36.5	58.5	33.5	61.5	4.5	0.5	27.5	72.5
Total	66.5	0.5	12	2.5	1.5	2.5	85.5	7.5	1	6	16.5	18.5	33.5	31.5	20	72.5	6	1.5	60.5	39.5

Table 28. Animal designs at Nämforsen, Ångermanland.

Area	AI2	AII2	AXI2	BI2	BII2	BXI2	CI2	CII2	CII4	CX2	DI2	DII2	BF2	CF2	AV	CV	Animal figures, total	Ships, total	%
I, River banks	2	36	3	–	4	–	–	120	–	1	–	1	–	2	3	4	176	65	*271*
II, Notön	1	61	–	1	8	1	–	62	1	–	2	8	–	–	1	–	146	139	*105*
III, Brådön	2	69	–	–	33	–	2	32	–	–	–	–	1	–	2	1	142	16	*887*
Total	5	166	3	1	45	1	2	214	1	1	2	9	1	2	6	5	464	220	*211*

Table 29. Type-defining elements of the quadruped designs at Nämforsen, Ångermanland.

Area	Total	Species										Body				Ears, horns, antlers				Legs	
		a	b	c	h	n	s	Qua-drupeds	F	O	V	A	B	C	D	I	II	X	XI	2	4
I, River banks	176	141	–	26	–	–	–	167	2	–	7	41	4	121	1	2	161	1	3	167	–
II, Notön	146	122	–	23	–	–	–	145	–	–	1	62	10	63	10	4	140	–	1	144	1
III, Brådön	142	116	–	22	–	–	–	138	1	–	3	71	33	34	–	4	134	–	–	138	–
Total	464	379	–	71	–	–	–	450	3	–	11	174	47	218	11	10	435	1	4	449	1

Table 30. Type-defining elements of the quadruped designs at Nämforsen, Ångermanland. Percentages.

Area	Species										Body				Ears, horns, antlers				Le
	a	b	c	h	n	s	Qua-drupeds	F	O	V	A	B	C	D	I	II	X	XI	2
I, River banks	80	–	15	–	–	–	95	1	–	4	24.5	2.5	72.5	0.5	1	96.5	0.5	2	100
II, Notön	83.5	–	16	–	–	–	99.5	–	–	0.5	43	7	43	7	3	96.5	–	0.5	99.5
III, Brådön	82	–	15.5	–	–	–	97.5	0.5	–	2	51.5	24	24.5	–	3	97	–	–	100
Total	81.5	–	15.5	–	–	–	97	0.5	–	2.5	38.5	10.5	48.5	2.5	2	96.5	0.5	1	99.5

Abbreviations

Aarb	Aarbøger for Nordisk Oldkyndighed og Historie (København)
Acta	Acta Archaeologica (København)
Acta Arch. Lund.	Acta Archaeologica Lundensia (Lund)
Ale	Ale. Historisk tidskrift för Skåneland (Lund)
Boh	Bohusläns Hembygdsförbunds Årsskrift (Uddevalla)
D	District
DKNVS	Det Kgl. Norske Videnskabers Selskab (Trondheim)
FM	Finskt Museum (Helsingfors)
Fv	Fornvännen (Stockholm)
Gbg	Göteborg
Inst. f.s.k.	Instituttet for sammenlignende kulturforskning (Oslo)
Khvn	København
Kuml	Kuml. Årbog for Jysk Arkæologisk Selskab (Århus)
Medd	Meddelanden från Lunds universitets historiska museum (Lund)
NAR	Norwegian Archaeological Review (Oslo)
Naturen	Naturen. Illustrert månedsskrift for populær naturvitenskap (Bergen)
S	South
SFT	Svenska Fornminnesföreningens Tidskrift (Stockholm)
SM	Soumen Museo (Helsingfors)
SMYA-FFT	Suomen Muinaismuistoyhdistyksen Aikakauskirja – Finska Fornminnesföreningens Tidskrift (Helsingfors)
Sthlm	Stockholm
Tor	Tor. Meddelanden från Institutionen för nordisk fornkunskap vid Uppsala universitet (Uppsala).
UFT	Upplands Fornminnesförenings Tidskrift (Uppsala)
VFÅ	Västmanlands Fornminnesförenings Tidskrift (Västerås)
Viking	Viking. Tidsskrift för norrøn arkeologi (Oslo)
Ymer	Ymer. Tidskrift utgiven av Svenska sällskapet för antropologi och geografi (Stockholm)

Bibliography

Åberg, L., 1839. Hällristningar från Bohuslän uti Sverige (Annaler for Nordisk Oldkyndighed, Khvn 1838–1839, p. 386–390).

Almgren, B., 1960. Hällristningar och bronsåldersdräkt. (Tor 6, 1960, p. 19–50).

— 1962. Den osynliga gudomen (i: Proxima Thule, hyllningsskrift till H. M. Konungen, Sthlm 1962, p. 53–71).

— 1964. Bronsåldersproblem i Norden (Tor 10, 1964, p. 149–160).

— 1970. Die Datierung der Schwedischen Felszeichnungen. (Actes du VIIe Congrès International des Sciences Préhistoriques et Protohistoriques, Prague 1966. Praha 1970, p. 674).

Almgren, O., 1912. Tanums härads fasta fornlämningar från bronsåldern. 1. Hällristningar (Bidrag till kännedom om Göteborgs och Bohusläns fornminnen och historia 8, Gbg 1906–1913, p. 473–575).

— 1927. Hällristningar och kultbruk (Sthlm 1927).

Althin, C.-A., 1945. Studien zu den bronzezeitlichen Felszeichnungen von Skåne (Lund 1945).

Anati, E., 1977. Methods of recording and analysing rock-engravings (Camunian Studies 7, Capo di Ponte 1977).

Arne, T. J., 1917. Ölands första kända bronsåldersristning (Fv 1917, p. 196–201).

Bakka, E., 1966. To helleristninger frå steinalderen i Hardanger (Viking 30, 1966, p. 77–95).

— 1971. Ei bronsealdervogn (Godbit fra samlingene, Historisk Museum, Bergen 1971).

— 1975. Bergkunst i barskogsbeltet i Sovjetsamveldet (Viking 1975, p. 95–124).

Baltzer, L., 1881–90. Hällristningar från Bohuslän, I. (Gbg 1881–90).

— 1891–1908. Hällristningar från Bohuslän, II. (Gbg 1891–1908).

Baudou, E., 1960. Die regionale und chronologische Einteilung der jüngeren Bronzezeit im Nordischen Kreis (Sthlm 1960).

— 1968. Forntida bebyggelse i Ångermanlands kustland (Örnsköldsvik 1968).

Bjørlykke, K. O., 1903. Helleristning ved Frones i Ullensvang (Naturen 27, 1903, p. 82–84).

Bjørn, A., 1916. Helleristningen paa Gurskø i Søndmør (Naturen 40, 1916, p. 379–382).

Bøe, Johs., 1932. Felszeichnungen im westlichen Norwegen. I. Die Zeichnungsgebiete in Vingen und Henøya (Bergen 1932).

— 1940. En helligdom med malte veggbilder i Hardanger (Viking 1940, p. 145–152).

Broholm, H. C., 1943. Danmarks Bronzealder, I (Khvn 1943).

— 1944. Danmarks Bronzealder, II (Khvn 1944).

— 1946. Danmarks Bronzealder, III (Khvn 1946).

— 1949. Danmarks Bronzealder, IV (Khvn 1949).

— 1952 A. Bronzealderfundet fra Grevensvænge (Aarb 1952, p. 41–55).

— 1952 B. Danske Oldsager, III. Ældre Bronzealder (Khvn 1952).

— 1953. Danske Oldsager, IV. Yngre Bronzealder (Khvn 1953).

Broholm, H. C., and *Hald, M.*, 1935. Danske Bronzealders Dragter (Nordiske Fortidsminder, II:5, Khvn 1935).

— 1939. Skrydstrupfundet (Nordiske Fortidsminder, III:2, Khvn 1939).

Brøndsted, J., 1966. Danmarks Oldtid, II. Bronzealderen (Khvn 1966).

Burenhult, G., 1972 A. Hällristningsdokumentation (Ale 3, 1972, p. 1–7).

— 1972 B. Rock carving chronology and rock carving ships with sails (Medd 1971–72, p. 151–162).

— 1973. The Rock Carvings of Götaland, II (Acta Arch. Lund., Ser. in 4°, No. 8, Lund 1973).

— 1979. Comments on Relations West Norway—Western Europe Documented in Petroglyphs, by E. N. Fett and P. Fett (NAR 12, 1979, p. 92–95).

— 1980. Götalands hällristningar, I (The Rock Carvings of Götaland, I. Theses and Papers in North European Archaeology, 10, Sthlm 1980).

Capelle, T., 1972. Felsbilder in Nordwestdeutschland. Eine Übersicht (Acta 43, 1972, p. 229–238).

Christie, W. F. K., 1837. Om Helle-Ristninger og andre Indhugninger i Klipper, især i Bergens Stift (Urda I, Bergen 1837, p. 91–97).

Claesson, C., 1932. Anteckningar om Dalslands hällristningar (Hembygden, Gbg 1932, p. 52–63).

Coll, A. L., 1901. Fra Helleristningernes Omraade (Foreningen til norske Fortidsmindesmærkers Bevaring. Aarsberetning 1901, p. 33–59).

— 1902. Fra Helleristningernes Omraade (Foreningen til norske Fortidsmindesmærkers Bevaring. Aarsberetning 1902, p. 106–140).

Cullberg, Kj., Nordbladh, J., and *Sjöberg, J. E.,* 1975. Tumlehed, Torslanda 216. Hällmålning, stenålder/bronsålder (FYND-rapporter 1975, p. 71–98).

Ekhoff, E., 1893. Hällristningar på Kinnekulle (SFT 8, 1891–93, p. 102–126).

Ekholm, G., 1916. De skandinaviska hällristningarna och deras betydelse (Ymer 1916, p. 275–308).

— 1918. En ny uppländsk hällristning (Fv 1918, p. 48–52).

— 1921 A. Undersökningar av uppländska hällristningar. Biskopskulla socken (UFT 36, 1921, p. 205–220).

— 1921 B. Studier i Upplands bebyggelsehistoria, II. Bronsåldern (Uppsala 1921).

— 1922. Om hällristningarnas kronologi och betydelse (Fv 1922, p. 239–259).

— 1931. Bronsålderns hällristningar (Nordisk Kultur 27, Sthlm 1931).

Engelstad, E. S., 1934. Østnorske ristninger og malinger av den arktiske gruppe (Inst. f.s.k., Ser. B, 26, Oslo 1934).

Erä-Esko, A., 1955. Rovaniemen kivikauden tutkimuksista (SM 1955, p. 84–99).

Europaeus, A., 1922. Fornfynd från Kyrkslätt och Esbo socknar (SMYA-FFT 32, 1922, p. 61–67).

Ewald, V., 1924. Hallands hällristningar (Vår Bygd, Halmstad 1924, p. 9–14).

Fett, P., 1939. Det forhistoriske Davik (in: J. Aaland: Nordfjord, Sandane 1939, p. 166–184).

Fett, E. and *P.*, 1941. Sydvestnorske helleristninger. Rogaland og Lista (Stavanger 1941).

— 1979. Relations West Norway—Western Europe documented in petroglyphs (NAR 12, 1979, p. 65–92).

Fredsjö, Å., 1947. Två hällristningsdetaljer (Göteborgs och Bohusläns fornminnesförenings tidskrift 1946–1947, p. 72–86).

— 1956. Göteborgstraktens hällristningar (Gbg 1956).

— 1966. Hällristningar i Kville, I (Boh 1966, p. 5–46).

— 1967. Hällristningar i Kville, II (Boh 1967, p. 57–79).

— 1968. Hällristningar i Kville, III (Boh 1968, p. 57–78).

— 1969. Hällristningar i Kville, IV (Boh 1969, p. 39–80).

— 1970. Hällristningar i Kville, V (Boh 1970, p. 39–81).

Fredsjö, Å., Janson, S., and *Moberg, C.-A.,* 1969. Hällristningar i Sverige (2nd ed., Oskarshamn 1969).

Fredsjö, Å., Nordbladh, J., and *Rosvall, J.,* 1971. Hällristningar i Kville härad i Bohuslän. Svenneby socken (Gbg 1971).

— 1975. Hällristningar i Kville härad i Bohuslän. Bottna socken (Gbg 1975).

Friesen, O. von, 1915. Undersökningar av uppländska hällristningar (UFT 30, 1915, p. 183–192).

Gjessing, G., 1932. Arktiske helleristninger i Nord-Norge (Inst. f.s.k., Ser. B, 21, Oslo 1932).

— 1935 A. Die Chronologie der Schiffsdarstellungen auf den Felsenzeichnungen zu Bardal, Trøndelag (Acta 6, 1935, p. 125–139).

— 1935 B. Veideristningen på Stein i Ringsaker, Hedmark (Universitetets Oldsaksamlings Årbok 1935–1936, p. 52–68).

— 1936. Nordenfjelske ristninger og malinger av den arktiske gruppe (Inst. f.s.k., Ser. B, 30, Oslo 1936).

— 1939. Østfolds jordbruksristninger. Idd, Berg og delvis Skjeberg (Inst. f.s.k., Ser. B, 37, Oslo 1939).

— 1945. Norges steinalder (Oslo 1945).

— 1970. Comments on Rock carvings in Østfold (NAR 3, 1970, p. 96–98).

Glob, P. V., 1951. Ard og plov i Nordens Oldtid (Århus 1951).

— 1969. Helleristninger i Danmark (Århus 1969).

Gräslund, B., 1964. Bronsålderns krumsvärd och frågan om deras ursprung (Tor 10, 1964, p. 285–308).

Gurina, N., 1956. Oleneostrovskij magiluik (Materialy i issledovanija po Archeologii SSSR, 47, Moskva 1956).

Hagen, A., 1965. Rock Carvings in Norway (Oslo 1965).

— 1967. Norges oldtid (Oslo 1967).

— 1969. Studier i vestnorsk bergkunst. Ausevik i Flora (Bergen 1969).

— 1970. Comments on Rock Carvings in Østfold (NAR 3, 1970, p. 105–112).

Hallström, G., 1917. Notiser om hällristningar i södra delen av Göteborgs och Bohus län (Fv 1917, p. 115–126).

— 1929. Dalslands hällristningar (i: Skoog, D. och Thedin, K., Dalsland, Uppsala 1929, p. 188–199).

— 1938. Monumental Art of Northern Europe from the Stone Age I. The Norwegian Localities (Sthlm 1938).

— 1952. Hällmålningarna i Kyrkslätts socken, Finland (i: Arkeologiska forskningar och fynd, Sthlm 1952, p. 397–409).

— 1960. Monumental Art of Northern Sweden from the Stone Age (Sthlm 1960).

Hasselrot, P., och *Ohlmarks, Å.,* 1966. Hällristningar (Sthlm 1966).

Holmberg, A. E., 1848. Skandinaviens hällristningar (Sthlm 1848).

Hultkrantz, Å., 1965. Type of religion in the arctic hunting cultures. A religio-ecological approach (in: Hunting and Fishing, Luleå 1965, p. 265–318).

— 1975. Ekologiska perspektiv på arktiska och subarktiska jägarreligioner (in: Jakt och fiske, Luleå 1975, p. 363–378).

Janson, S., 1960. Hällristningen vid Tuna i Bälinge (Tor 1960, p. 51–57).

Janson, S., and *Hvarfner, H.,* 1960. Från Norrlandsälvar och fjällsjöar (Sthlm 1960).

Janson, S., and *Westman, D.,* 1966. Hällristningar vid Fiskeby (Sthlm 1966).

Janson, S. and *B.,* 1980. Hällristningar vid Nämforsen (Sthlm 1980).

Jansson, S. B. F., 1963. Runinskrifter i Sverige (Uppsala 1963).

Johansen, E., 1944 A. Nyoppdagete jordbruksristninger med spor av maling (Naturen 68, 1944, p. 298–303).

— 1944 B Nyoppdagete helleristninger ved Begby i Borge, Østfold (Viking 1944, p. 99–120).

— 1970. Med hevet hånd (Kuml 1970, p. 171–188).

Johansen, O. S., 1969. Nordiske petroglyfer. Terminologi, kronologi, kontaktpunkter utenfor Norden (Universitetets Oldsaksamlings Årbok 1969, p. 220–234).

Kivikoski, E., 1964. Finlands förhistoria (Helsingfors 1964).

Kjellén, E., 1939. Nypptäckta hällristningar i sydvästra Uppland (UFT 46, 1939, p. 81–95).

— 1960. Något om Enköpingstraktens hällristningar (Tor 1960, p. 5–18).

Kjellén, E., and *Hyenstrand. Å.,* 1976. Upplands hällristningar (Sthlm 1976).

— 1977. Hällristningar och bronsålderssamhälle i sydvästra Uppland (UFT 49, 1977).

Kjellin, H., 1940. "Wärmeland i sitt ämne och i sin upodling". Jubileumsutställning (Värmland förr och nu 37–38, 1939–40, p. 127–422).

Kjellmark, K., and *Lindsten, O.,* 1909. Nyupptäckta hällristningar vid Hjulatorp i Bergs socken, Kronobergs län (Fv 1909, p. 187–194).

Kühn, H., and *Arbman, H.,* 1955. Europas förhistoriska klippkonst (Uddevalla 1955).

Lange, E. de, 1912. Ornerte heller i norske bronsealdersgrave (Bergens museums Årbok 1912, nr 4).

Larsson, L., 1974. The Fogdarp find. A hoard from the Late Bronze Age (Medd 1973–74, p. 169–238).

Leijonhufvud, M., 1908. Nyupptäckt hällristning på Kinnekulle (Fv 1908, p. 87–92).

Lidén, O., 1938. Hällgröpningsstudier i anslutning till nya sydsvenska fynd (Lund 1938).

Lisch, G. F. C., 1838. Metallbeschlag eines Histhorns von Wismar (Jahresbericht des Vereins für mecklenburgische Geschichte und Altertumskunde 3, p. 67–77).

Lomborg, E., 1959. Donauländische Kulturbeziehungen und die relative Chronologie der frühen nordischen Bronzezeit (Acta 30, 1959, p. 51–146).

Luho, V., 1962. Klippmålningen vid Juusjärvi (FM 1962, p. 61–71).

— 1968. En hällmålning i Taipalsaari (FM 1968, p. 33–39).

Lund, H., 1934. En eldre bronsealders ornert gravhelle fra Rege i Håland på Jæren (Stavanger Museums Årshefte 1933–34, p. 49–53).

Magnusson, G., 1979. Forntid i Tjust i ljuset av den senaste fornminnesinventeringen (Tjustbygden 36, 1979, p. 13–27).

Malmer, M. P., 1949. Gerumsmanteln (Svensk uppslagsbok, Bd 11, Malmö 1949, p. 597).

— 1957. Pleionbegreppets betydelse för studiet av förhistoriska innovationsförlopp (SMYA-FFT 58, 1957, p. 160–184).

— 1962. Jungneolithische Studien (Acta Arch. Lund., Ser. in 8°, 2, 1962).

— 1963. Metodproblem inom järnålderns konsthistoria (Methodological problems in the history of art during the Scandinavian Iron Age) (Acta Arch. Lund., Ser. in 8°, 3, 1963).

— 1968. De kronologiska grundbegreppen (Fv 1968, p. 81–91).

— 1970. Bronsristningar (Kuml 1970, p. 189–210).

— 1974. Hällristningsforskning och modern arkeologi (in: Nya vetenskapliga perspektiv, Sthlm 1974, p. 71–86).

— 1975. The rock carvings at Nämforsen, Ångermanland, as a problem of maritime adaptation and circumpolar interrelations (in: Prehistoric Maritime Adaptations of the Circumpolar Zone, Chicago 1975, p. 41–46).

— 1979. Comments on Relations West Norway—Western Europe documented in petroglyphs (NAR 12, 1979, p. 95–97).

Malmer, M. P., and *Burenhult, G.,* 1972. Ett museum som projekt och projekt i museet (in: Forntid för framtid, Sthlm 1972, p. 154–161).

Mandt, G., 1972. Bergbilder i Hordaland. En undersøkelse av bildenes sammensetning, deres naturmiljø og kulturmiljø (Bergen 1972).

— 1974. Review of Olav Sverre Johansen: Nordiske petroglyfer (NAR 7, 1974, p. 86–88).

Marstrander, S., 1941. Jordbruk og bergskurd (Viking 59, 1941, p. 29–50).

— 1950. Det første helleristningsfund fra Gauldal (DKNVS Forhandlinger 23, nr 18).

— 1953. New Rock-carvings of Bronze-age Type in the District of Trøndelag, Norway (Congrès international des Sciences Préhistoriques et Protohistoriques. Actes de la IIIᵉ Session Zürich 1950, Zürich 1953, p. 242–247).

— 1963. Østfolds jordbruksristninger. Skjeberg (Inst. f.s.k. Ser. B, 53, Trondheim 1963).

— 1966. Nye resultater i utforskningen av bronsealderens helleristninger (DKNVS Årbok 1966, p. 103–120).

— 1971. Reply to the comments on Rock Carvings in Østfold (NAR 4, 1971, p. 51–56).

— 1979. Comments on Relations West Norway—Western Europe documented in petroglyphs (NAR 12, 1979, p. 97–100).

Mathiassen, Th., 1957. Endnu et Krumsværd (Aarb 1957, p. 38–55).

Meinander, C. F., 1954 A. Die Kiukaiskultur (SMYA-FFT 53, 1954).

— 1954 B. Die Bronzezeit in Finnland (SMYA-FFT) 54, 1954).

Moberg, C.-A., 1957. Vilka hällristningar är från bronsåldern? (Tor 1957, p. 49–64).

— 1970. Regional och global syn på hällristningar (Kuml 1970, p. 223–232).

Montelius, O., 1900. Ett märkligt fynd från Södermanland (SFT 10, 1900, p. 189–204)

— 1917. Minnen från vår forntid (Sthlm 1917).

Nordbladh, J., 1980. Glyfer och rum. Kring hällristningar i Kville (Gbg 1980).

Nordén, A., 1917. Hällristningarnas kronologi och betydelse (Ymer 37, 1917, p. 57–83).

— 1925 A. Östergötlands bronsålder (Linköping 1925).

— 1925 B. Brandskogs-skeppet (Fv 1925, p. 276–391).

Nordin, F., 1911. Gotlands första kända hällristning. Vid Hägvide i Lärbro sn (Fv 1911, p. 144–152).

Ojonen, S., 1973. Hällmålningarna vid sjöarna Kotojärvi och Märkjärvi i Iitti (FM 1973, p. 35–46).

Oldeberg, A., 1933. Det nordiska bronsåldersspännets historia (Stockholm 1933).

Olsén, P., 1965. Norrköpingstraktens fornminnen (in: Norrköpings historia, I, Sthlm 1965).

Ørsnes, M., Borbjergfundet (Aarb 1958, p. 1–107).

Petersen, Th., 1925. Helleristningerna på Okkenhaug i Frol (Nordtrøndelag Historielag. Aarbok for 1925, p. 26–34).

— 1926. Nye fund fra det nordenfjelske Norges helleristningsområde (SMYA-FFT 36, 1926, p. 23–44).

— 1933. Litt om den eldste bosetning i Sunndalen (Årsskrift for Nordmør Historielag 1933, p. 53–63).

Post, L., von, Walterstorff, E. von, and *Lindqvist, S.,* 1925. Bronsåldersmanteln från Gerumsberget (Sthlm 1924–25).

Ramskou, Th., 1952. Découverte nouvelle de signes cupelliformes et de roues solaires dans des tombaux de l'age de bronze (Acta 23, 1952, p. 132–138).

Raudonikas, W. J., 1936. Les gravures rupestres des bords du lac Onéga et de la mer Blanche, I. Les gravures rupestres du lac Onéga (Leningrad 1936).

— 1938. Les gravures rupestres des bords du lac Onéga et de la mer Blanche, II. Les gravures rupestres de la mer Blanche (Leningrad 1938).

Rekstad, J., 1910. Helleristninger i Herand i Hardanger (Naturen 34, 1910, p. 48–51).

Rostholm, H., 1972. Danske helleristninger og deres forhold til de øvrige nordiske helleristninger fra bronzealderen (Holstebro museums årsskrift 1971–72, p. 1–31).

Rygh, K., 1908. Helleristninger af den sydskandinaviske type i det nordenfjelske Norge (DKNVS Skrifter 1908, No 10).

— 1910. Arkæologiske undersøgelser 1910 (DKNVS Skrifter 1910, no. 6).

— 1913. En ny helleristning i Øvre Stjørdalen (DKNVS Skrifter 1913, no. 5).

Salomonsson, B., 1958. Hällristningar i Blekinge (Blekingeboken 1958, p. 9–26).

Sarvas, P., 1969. Die Felsmalerei von Astuvansalmi (SM 1969, p. 5–33).

— 1970. Hällmålningen vid Noux Långträsk (FM 1970, p. 12–16).

Sarvas, P., and *Taavitsainen, J. P.*, 1975. Käköveden kalliomaalaukset (Kotiseuto 1975, p. 133–138).

— 1976. Kalliomaalauksia Lemiltä ja Ristiinasta (SM 1976, p. 30–52).

Savvateev, J. A., 1967. O novych petroglifach Karelii (Sovetskaja archeologija 1967, 2, p. 3–21).

— 1968. Petroglify novoj Zalavrugi (Sovetskaja archeologija 1968, 1, p. 134–157).

Schetelig, H., 1908. Helleristninger paa Støle i Søndhordaland (Naturen 32, 1908, p. 343–348).

Schnittger, B., 1911. En hällristning i Västergötland (Fv 1911, p. 196–203).

— 1922. En hällristning vid Berga-Tuna i Södermanland jämte några allmänna synpunkter på hällristningsproblemen (Fv 1922, p. 77–112).

Schwantes, G., 1939. Die Vorgeschichte Schleswig-Holsteins (Neumünster 1939).

Simonsen, P., 1958. Arktiske helleristninger i Nord-Norge, II (Inst. f.s.k., Ser. B, 49, Oslo 1958).

— 1961. Varanger-funnene, II (Tromsø 1961).

— 1978. New elements for evaluating the origin and end of northern Scandinavian rock art (Inst. f.s.k., Ser. A, 29, Oslo 1978, p. 31–36).

Simonsson, H., 1960. En nyfunnen hällristning i Munktorp sn (VFÅ 1960, p. 5–19).

Skjelsvik, E., and *Straume, E.*, 1957. Austrheimsteinen i Nordfjord. Et nytt bidrag til dateringen (Universitetet i Bergen. Årbok 1957. Historisk-antikvarisk rekke, 1).

Taavitsainen, J. P., 1978. Hällmålningarna – en ny synvinkel på Finlands förhistoria (Antropologi i Finland, 4, 1978, p. 179–195).

Welinder, S., 1974. A study on the Scanian rock carvings by quantitative methods (Medd 1973–74, p. 244–275).

Wihlborg, A., 1972. Hällristningar och järnåldersgravar. En preliminär beskrivning av en arkeologisk undersökning vid Sagaholm i Jönköping (Småländska kulturbilder 1972, p. 7–19).

— 1978. Sagaholm. A Bronze Age barrow with rock-carvings (Medd 1977–1978, p. 111–128).